HOMER'S ODYSSEY

HOMER'S ODYSSEY

AN ILLUSTRATED RETELLING

Adapted by Barry B. Powell
Illustrated by Joanna Lisowiec

RIVERSIDE PRESS

Contents

Introduction

The *Odyssey* is the second oldest work of Western literature, and was likely composed around 820 BCE. The older work is the *Iliad*, which precedes the Odyssey by some years. Both were composed by a man named Homer, about whom almost nothing is known. He was an *aoidos*, a singer of epic tales, who composed songs in a special metre with repeated epithets and phrases.

As far as we can tell, such a singer could neither read nor write. He learned his craft as a child, sitting at the feet of a master. Then he became an entertainer, performing in the houses of men of power and at public gatherings. He preserved stories about the families of those he entertained, especially stories about the Trojan war.

Homer was an *aoidos*, but he was no ordinary *aoidos*. He swept up old stories and hundreds of names of men and women, gods and monsters, all stored in his capacious memory. The reader is astonished at the plethora of names in Homer's poems. An ordinary *aoidic* performance at a banquet would most likely have been a song of a few hundred lines. Homer's poems run to more than ten thousand lines each, and the scribe who recorded them has instructed the poet not to spare any details.

The main story of the *Odyssey* is an old one, concerning the triumph of life over death. The hero is the trickster of popular lore, Odysseus *polutropos*, that is, "Odysseus of many turns". He is flexible; he bends his intelligence to the problems at hand. He descends to the netherworld, the House of Hades, and returns to this world to restore civic order. He defeats many monsters who want to eat him, as death devours all. People constantly declare that Odysseus is dead – Telemachus, Penelope, the suitors – yet to everyone's surprise, he returns to life.

If Odysseus is the figure of life in this struggle, the figure of death comes in two forms: the chaotic and cannibalistic monsters, and the chaotic power of the sea. Early on in his travels, Odysseus blinds Poseidon's son, the Cyclops Polyphemus, and earns the god's enmity. Poseidon is the sea and the sea is death, the enemy and the cause of the hero's suffering. Even Poseidon's own mortal relatives, the Phaecians, are not spared the god's vengeance when they presume to aid Odysseus on his journey home.

Odysseus' allies in the battle against these forces are justice-loving gods. Throughout the tale, Odysseus receives assistance from Athena, and Zeus nods his approval. It is a pious poem, then, in which justice prevails in a moral universe, presided over by Zeus. In the opening scene on Olympus, Zeus complains that people blame the gods for their suffering, but in reality their pain proceeds logically from their own decisions. The suitors simply do not respect the gods or the moral order. This is their decision. Obviously they must perish.

Odysseus and his men are not completely innocent, of course. Their great crime, announced in the opening lines of the poem, is that they eat the Cattle of the Sun – something they are forbidden to do, and are warned against by Circe. Stories often turn on this kind of violated taboo: whatever you do, don't do this! And yet, tragic drama demands that the taboo be broken, and the heroes suffer the consequences. Odysseus is punished, but he escapes destruction because, as the story is quick to highlight, he did not himself participate in the slaughter of the cattle.

A key element of morality in Homer's Greece – and a key divider between heroes and villains in the *Odyssey* – is the custom of *xenia*, the way you are expected to treat a wandering stranger. Members of the elite recognize members of their own class and treat them well, and are even respectful of beggars. For the gods sometimes take on the form of human beings, and that stranger in rags could be a deity in disguise!

Eating is an important part of *xenia*. Again and again Homer tells us that characters killed an animal, gave a sample to the gods and shared the rest with their guests. Ordinarily, when an aristocrat travels he is lavishly entertained at a banquet. The Cyclops, instead of offering Odysseus a meal, as would a decent host, makes a meal of his men, a grotesque violation of *xenia* and a symbol of the Cyclops' savagery. The suitors, similarly, parody this custom by demanding constant banquets at their host's expense, while abusing genuine guests such as the disguised Odysseus.

The other crucial element of *xenia* is the giving of gifts. At very least, the traveller is offered a cloak and tunic, from the rough clothing offered by the swineherd Eumaeus, to the exquisite robe Helen gives to Telemachus. The wealthiest kings and nobles also offer greater treasures to their guests, as a mark of highest esteem. So moral status in Homer's world is bound up with virtuous gifts of food, clothing, and fine presents of metalwork and woven cloth.

The custom of *xenia* is not just a matter for the noble classes. In fact, a prominent theme in the *Odyssey* is the varying relationship between social class and virtue. The swineherd Eumaeus was born a prince, but is now a provincial slave tending swine. Yet his hospitality towards the disguised Odysseus stands in stark contrast to the suitors' behaviour, and he becomes Odysseus' most trusted companion, and a critical ally in his victory. Loyalty and obedience to the will of the gods replace class solidarity in the *Odyssey*, and the struggle against the suitors can be viewed as a battle between arrogant aristocrats, on the one hand, and rightful power supported by the will of the people on the other. Such lessons cannot have been lost on Homer's original audience.

Homer's poems also mark a breakthrough in literary expression. Before Homer, there were epics written in Egyptian hieroglyphics and Mesopotamian cuneiform, but they seem crude today in comparison to Homer's poetry. Part of that is due to the scripts used to record them. The *Iliad* and the *Odyssey* were first written down in the late 9th century BCE. They were inscribed in a specially adapted alphabet known as Ugaritic cuneiform. Previous forms of the alphabet did not allow for the nuances of sound that capture the rhythm and music of Homer's verse. The scribe had to create a new way of differentiating characters, by individual sounds rather than by syllables, in order to record Homer's work. This new system laid the foundations for modern alphabets: a form of writing that can be recombined to record any spoken word, and interpreted by any reader, not just a select few.

This flexibility of language allows Homer's characters to reflect all the depth and subtlety of spoken-word poetry. Figures in other myths at the time, such as Gilgamesh or Goliath, are comparatively characterless and formulaic. But in the *Odyssey*, we have complex, literary personalities, flawed and deeply human.

Telemachus is the teenage son of Odysseus, humiliated and shamed by the crowd of suitors, all young men, who insult him and destroy his wealth. He is short with his mother, whom he sees as indecisive and responsible for the suitors' depredations. He goes on an adventure looking for his father but discovers his own worth. In the end Telemachus proves he is his father's son.

Penelope is always weeping, even though it's been twenty years since her husband left to go to the Trojan War. She is at least forty years old, but still so beautiful that, when she enters the hall, the suitors burn with sexual desire. Penelope is the archetype of the faithful wife who remains true, no matter how she is tempted. She is also extremely clever, putting off the suitors through the trick of unravelling her weaving, instigating the contest of the bow and even testing Odysseus with intimate knowledge of their bed.

Homer's depth of characterization extends well beyond the main cast. He loves telling incidental stories, such as the false tales of Odysseus' origin on Crete, or the episode with the rival beggar, Irus. Homer has fun with drunken tale-telling by Menelaüs and Helen over the punch bowl in Sparta, and winks at Nestor's rambling accounts of the Trojan War. These tales do not advance the main story, and scholars once thought that they were insertions by later poets, but Homer likes to slow down his narrative. That's his style, and it leaves us today with a wonderfully complex and humane picture of Homeric society.

The significance of Homer's *Odyssey* is hard to overstate. After nearly 3,000 years, it still stands as a landmark of literary culture, at the unique inception of alphabetic writing and naturalistic storytelling. It is also a fine story in its own right: a tale of gods and monsters, storms and Cyclops, witches and whirlpools, full of epic heroism and adventure, but also family, faithfulness and the universal longing for home. It is a tale well worth revisiting to this day.

Book 1

THE STORY BEGINS

Oh Muse, help me sing the tale of Odysseus, man of resourcefulness, courage and wisdom, and his epic journey home from Troy!

The war was finally over. The city of Troy was burned to the ground, its warriors dead or exiled, its women enslaved. The Greek heroes – those who survived the ten-year siege – had returned home, some to lives of peace, some to violence and tragedy.

All Greece's heroes, that is, except one: Odysseus. He was still trapped on an island far from his homeland, held captive by the nymph Calypso.

In his palace high on snow-capped Mount Olympus, Zeus, the father of the gods, was pondering the fates of mortals. Zeus' daughter, wise Athena, came to him to plead Odysseus' case.

"Mighty father, Odysseus still languishes on a distant island, where Calypso tries to make him her husband. He yearns for his home, Ithaca and for his faithful wife Penelope. Poor Odysseus – he has always been so attentive in his sacrifices to you, yet he has been wandering for longer than any other Greek warrior."

"Ah, Odysseus," mused Zeus. "I have not forgotten him, and I bear him no ill will. But he enraged my brother Poseidon when he blinded his son, the Cyclops Polyphemus. It is Poseidon's anger that keeps Odysseus trapped so far from all that he loves. You are right: it is time my brother forgot his grudge and joined the rest of us in helping Odysseus return."

Athena glowed with pleasure at Zeus' words. "Mighty father, I beg you to send Hermes to Calypso at once, to set Odysseus free. Meanwhile, I will go to Ithaca. His wife Penelope is surrounded by arrogant suitors. They believe her husband dead and so squat in his palace, like parasites. Odysseus will not be able to reclaim his home without some help." She grasped her mighty bronze-tipped spear, the terror of all enemies of the gods. "I will speak to Odysseus' son, Telemachus, and prepare him for his father's return."

At Odysseus' palace in Ithaca, the scene was squalid. Penelope's uninvited suitors sprawled among the remains of their latest feast, lazing on the skins of slaughtered oxen, squabbling over games of dice and demanding that the servants bring them ever more wine and meat from the palace stores.

Telemachus sat apart, keeping uneasy watch over the unwelcome guests. A boy of sixteen, with no father around to train him in battle, he could not hold his own against so many grown men. But he bitterly resented their arrogance and the way they insulted his family. Every day, he longed to see his father come home and drive the invaders away. He gazed through the palace gates, imagining Odysseus striding up the path, leading his faithful soldiers with their bronze swords and spears flashing in the sunlight.

The sun dazzled his eyes for a moment, and when his vision cleared, he saw that there was indeed a warrior at the gates. There stood a tall stranger clad in rich robes, bearing a heavy spear. The suitors were too ill-mannered to move; Telemachus, however, started forward to greet the visitor in a civilized fashion, offering hospitality.

"Greetings, stranger, and welcome to our house. Please, sit with me and eat, then tell me how we may help you."

He led Athena in her disguise into the hall, placing her spear in a large rack filled with Odysseus' own weapons. Then he instructed a slave to set out a chair and a footrest, keeping a distance from the suitors so that their uproar would not ruin the stranger's pleasure in a meal. He sat down next to his guest. He wanted to talk to him about his father.

A handmaid brought in cool water in golden pitchers and poured it over their hands into a silver basin. She set up tables for them and served out savoury loaves of bread and delicious sweets. A carver brought in all kinds of meats, and a slave filled goblets with wine.

The suitors also came to dine now, sitting in rows beside low tables. Slaves moved among them, washing their hands and bringing out more steaming loaves. Broad cups were topped up with wine, and the suitors became raucous. Their fancy turned to entertainment – singing and dancing, the best part of a good feast. A slave placed a lyre in the hands of the minstrel, Phemius, and the suitors fiercely insisted that he regale them with stories. Phemius struck a few chords.

Telemachus leaned in close to his visitor so the suitors could not overhear. "Stranger, I hope you don't mind if I speak frankly? These men just gorge and sing and dance. Everything they consume belongs to a man who will never return! My father, Odysseus, is dead. His white bones lie on some shore, where the waves roll them on the sand. He will never return to take vengeance on these men! My father is dead, gone!

"I wish I knew more about him. Tell me, have you been here before, visiting my father? I remember he hosted many guests when I was small. Who are you, and where do you come from? Where is your city, and who are your parents? How did you get here? Who were the sailors that brought you? I don't believe you came on foot!"

"I am Mentês, lord among the Taphians," Athena said. "I have moored my ship in the harbour. I'm sailing west across the sea to buy copper, with iron in my ship for trade. Your father and I were old friends – you can ask Odysseus' own father, your grandfather Laertes, about me. I hear he lives a wretched life on the mountains cultivating just a tiny patch of land, cared for by an old woman.

"I had heard that your father had come back, but I see I was wrong. Perhaps he lies in a prison somewhere, held by barbarians. The gods seem against him, but I'm sure he will return; he is daring and full of schemes.

"But tell me, are you really Odysseus' son? You look like him. Your eyes are similar, and the slant of your brow. Your father and I were often together, until he left for Troy with the Achaeans. I have not seen Odysseus since then, nor he me."

"Well, Mother says he's my father, at least," Telemachus replied. "I mean, who really knows who his parents are? She told me he was my father, but I wish were I was born to a man who died at peace among his possessions, loved by all, rather than to the unluckiest man who ever lived."

"Be happy that you come from such a fine family, and that your sons will too," Athena answered. "But what is going on in this place? Is this some kind of wedding party? It's clear these men have not brought their own food. Any man would be outraged to see what's going on. Frankly, I am!"

"Our house was rich once, while Odysseus lived here," Telemachus said. "But the gods have made him disappear. I would not be as distressed if he had died at Troy in his friends' arms and received a decent burial. Instead, he's disappeared. Now the princes from all the nearby islands, and Ithaca too, are courting my mother. She can't say yes or no; meanwhile, the suitors are eating up my fortune. I'll be ruined!"

"A horrific situation," Athena said, angered by his words. "You do need your father. I wish he were here now. He'd take a stand at the outer gate, wearing armour and holding a shield and two spears, just how I saw him

when he stopped by my house many years ago. He was looking for poison for his arrows, and my father gave him some. I wish he were here and that he would kill these men. That would be a fine marriage for them!

"Listen to me. Tomorrow, gather together the suitors and tell them to leave. To go home. As for your mother, send her to her father's house in Sparta. Let her marry there, if she truly believes your father to be dead. She will have a splendid wedding, fitting for a woman of her status. And as for you, find oarsmen and prepare yourself for a journey to discover what you can about your father. Find out if he's still alive. Maybe someone will know something.

"Cross the seas first to Pylos. That's where old Nestor rules, the oldest Achaean to fight at Troy. Then go to Sparta and find Menelaüs, Agamemnon's brother. Menelaüs was the last to return from Troy, and he may know something.

"If you discover that Odysseus is dead, you must come back to Ithaca and build a burial mound. Say prayers over the mound and give your mother to someone in marriage. When you've done these things, then decide how best to kill these men – with cunning, or quite brazenly. You are not a child anymore. Be valiant like your father! But now I must go down to my ship because my men are waiting. Do what I say!"

"Thank you for the advice, Mentês," Telemachus answered. "You've spoken as a father to his son. I will do what you say. But come, take a warm bath and eat your fill. Then you may go with good cheer to your ship. And I will give you a gift, something to remember me by, that will bind us together as friends."

"Thank you, my son, but I must not delay. As for the gift, I will pick it up on the way back; we will be friends forever, and I'll have a gift for you."

So spoke Athena, and then she flew upwards like a bird. Telemachus was astounded, even though he had suspected that his visitor was no ordinary being. Filled with confidence, he got up to mingle with the suitors.

The men were silent for once, spellbound by Phemius' melodious song telling of the disasters that befell many of the Greeks on their journeys home from Troy. Penelope, the daughter of Icarius, heard the lovely music and came down the stairway from her chamber, accompanied by two handmaids. She stood by the pillar near the hallway, covered her face with a veil and, with tears in her eyes, spoke:

"Phemius, you know the songs of noble men and the great deeds they do, and your tales make them great. Sing one of these songs, please, and let these men sit silently and drink their wine. Stop this song about horrible Troy! I see my husband's face before me even as I speak."

But Telemachus interrupted: "Mother, for the sake of all that is good, let the poor man sing what song he wants! It's not his fault! It's Zeus, I daresay, who gives each man what he deserves. You can't blame the singer for the evil fate of the Achaeans. This song is his most recent, and so he likes it. Just listen and bear up. Your Odysseus wasn't the only man who lost his happy homecoming. Now go to your room, Mother. Take your handmaidens with you; work at the loom. This song is for men! For all men, yes, but above all for me, because I am the master of this house!"

So spoke Telemachus, from the grief of his own heart.

Penelope was stung by his words. She turned quickly and went upstairs to her chamber where she sat down and wept bitter tears for the loss of her cherished husband, until sleep overcame her. Downstairs, the suitors laughed and mocked her, and each man said he would love to sleep with this woman.

"Suitors of my mother!" Telemachus addressed the men. "For now, we feast, drink and listen to this pleasant singer. Tomorrow morning, however, we will gather in the town square. Understand this: you must leave this palace forever! Go to another feast in another house! Or, if you think it just to carry on draining my father's wealth, stay! And I will call on Zeus and the other gods to see that you perish in my halls."

His bold words amazed them.

"Good speech," said Antinoüs, a leader among the suitors. "Are the gods coaching you? I hope that Zeus never grants you the rule of Ithaca."

"Well Antinoüs, there are plenty of men in Ithaca who could be king. Let one of them do it, since Odysseus is dead. But king or not, I am the master of this house! And I will preside over the property that my father has left to me."

Then Eurymachus, another of the suitors' ringleaders, spoke. "I believe it's up to the gods who becomes king. As for your possessions, keep them, and your house too. I don't think anyone will take anything by force. We Ithacans won't allow it. But tell me, Telemachus, who was that man just now who sat by you there in the dark? Who was he? Did he come with news of your father's return, or on some other matter? I mean, first he was here and then he was gone, giving us no chance to get to know him. Judging by his dress, he was no base fellow."

"I put no faith in reports of my father's return," said Telemachus, "for I know he will never come back. That he is lost. We pay no attention to prophecies that my mother hears from soothsayers. That man was a friend of my father, from Taphos. His name is Mentês, powerful among the Taphians."

So spoke Telemachus, but in his heart he knew his guest was no mortal.

The suitors returned to their partying as they danced and listened to the singing until night fell. Then each man went to his house. Telemachus walked into the open courtyard, his aged faithful slave Eurycleia carrying torches before him. Eurycleia had nursed Telemachus as a baby. Odysseus' father Laertes bought her years ago, paying twenty cattle.

Telemachus' room was situated off the courtyard. He opened the door and went in and sat on the bed with its base of tight cords. Eurycleia took his white tunic from him and hung it on a peg, then left. She shut the door behind her, latching it with a silver bar.

All night long Telemachus could not sleep, thinking of the journey that lay ahead of him.

Book 2

TELEMACHUS PLANS A JOURNEY

The next day, Telemachus rose at the crack of dawn. He donned his tunic and strapped his bronzed sword over his shoulders. Onto his feet he bound golden sandals. Then he took up his spear and strode from the room. He looked like a young god.

Telemachus summoned his slaves and instructed them to call an assembly. Before long, the Ithacan noblemen and all the townspeople were gathered together in the town square. Telemachus made his way through the throng, accompanied by two handsome dogs. Assertively he took his place at the stone seat that had always been his father's place. A herald placed the speaker's staff in his hands, giving him the floor.

"Sirs," he said, "I am the one who has convened this assembly. The issue I wish to raise concerns my own household. I have suffered grievously twice over. My father, Odysseus, formerly King here in Ithaca, kind to his people, is dead. Now an even greater evil has befallen me: the young men of Ithaca court my mother, his widow, and drive me to despair. They don't behave as noblemen ought, visiting her father Icarius in Sparta to request her hand in marriage. They don't allow him to choose her the best suitor, or arrange a splendid wedding. No, instead they amuse themselves at my expense, squatting in my house, slaughtering my cattle, my sheep and my swine, and downing my father's wine until there is nothing left. I am close to ruin. And by myself I am powerless to turn them out. You should all feel the disgrace of this terrible situation! Shame on all you noblemen for letting this come to pass! Do you not fear the righteous anger of Olympian Zeus and the other gods? It would be better if you all stole from me, for at least then I could go to each of your houses and beg back what you had taken! Shame, shame, shame for what you have done!"

Telemachus burst into sobs and dashed the staff to the ground. The nobles were filled with pity for the boy and said nothing for a long time.

One of the suitors, Antinoüs, finally spoke, in his arrogant way. "Quite a speech, young man. But don't blame us. Your mother is the problem. She sends secret little messages to each suitor, suggesting how he might find special favour with her – but she's been doing this for four years now, and still hasn't decided whom she wants. She plays tricks on us. She set up a loom in the hall to weave a shroud, ready for when your grandfather Laertes dies. She told us she would marry once she had finished it.

"She gave a fine little speech: 'Dear suitors, since Odysseus is dead, I must marry again, but be patient. First, I must finish this robe, a shroud for Laertes once cruel death strikes him down. The women of Ithaca would be ashamed to see a man of such wealth and power wanting for a shroud.'

"That's what she said. And we agreed to wait. And day by day she would weave at the loom – but each night, she would return by torchlight to undo her day's work. This went on for years, and it's only now, in the fourth year, that we've found out the truth, thanks to a slave. We caught her in the act and made her finish her weaving.

"Send your mother away, Telemachus. I'm serious. Send her to her father Icarius and have him choose a suitor, someone he likes, and make her decide too. She's skilled at weaving, a highly intelligent woman with a fine mind, blessed with great good sense. There's no one to equal her. But she is making a mistake. If she wants to continue her tricksy ways we'll stay where we are and keep eating you out of house and home. And we will *not* disperse until she marries the suitor she likes best."

"Antinoüs," Telemachus answered, "there is no way that I can turf out my own mother, who bore me and raised me! My father's away in some other land – if he's even alive! I can't send her back to her father. It's too much for me to pay back the dowry and Icarius would certainly do me harm. My mother would call down the Furies for vengeance and I would be hated by everyone. I can never do this! You don't *have* to stay at my house. Move around each other's houses! If you think it's acceptable to sponge off one man who can never take revenge, that's your choice. But I will call on Zeus and the gods so that retribution falls on you and you perish within my halls."

Just then, all-seeing Zeus sent down from a high mountain two powerful eagles that flew side by side, beating their mighty wings and soaring on the wind until they reached the town square, where they wheeled about. There they flapped their feathers savagely and eyed the men below with the look of death, and clawed one another with their talons, gouging their cheeks so that red blood flowed. Then they turned and flew away high above the town's houses. The Ithacans were astonished by the omen.

Halitherses, one of the elders and a friend of Odysseus, knew about the flight of birds and spoke up.

"Listen to me, men of Ithaca, and listen well," he said. "I address the suitors above all. A great calamity awaits you. Odysseus will soon be here! He is already nearby, and slaughter and death are in prospect for you. I do not say these things in ignorance. When Odysseus left for the war twenty years ago I prophesied he would be gone for twenty years and then return. Now this is coming to pass."

"Curse you, old man," said the handsome suitor Eurymachus. "Get off home and prophesy to your children! Tell them there may be harm in the offing. I believe I know a thing or two, and I say that birds fly every which way all the time. It means nothing. Odysseus is dead, far away – and if only you'd died with him."

Telemachus spoke up calmly now. "Eurymachus, and the rest of you, I shall say no more on this matter. I ask only that you give me a ship and twenty companions so that I may cross the sea to Sparta and to Pylos to learn if anyone has heard news of my father. If I discover that he is alive and someday will come home, then I can endure this situation for a year. But if I hear that he is dead, I will return to my beloved land, build a burial mound and perform funeral rites. Then I shall give my mother to a husband."

He sat down. Mentor, a friend of Odysseus, stood up. When Odysseus left for Troy he entrusted Mentor with the care of his house and instructed the staff to show him respect.

"Let no sceptred king ever be kind and just!" said good-natured Mentor. "Let him be harsh and show no justice, seeing how everyone has forgotten how gentle and kind Odysseus was, like a father to his people. It's one thing for the suitors to go on with their violent behaviour – I don't care if they risk their own lives devouring the house of a man they assume will never return. But I am outraged at the rest of you who sit in silence, raising no protest and allowing the suitors to act in this way, even though you are many and they are few."

"You're an old fool, Mentor!" said the suitor Leiocritus, standing up. "This is insane! Saying that we should be stopped from our feasting and making merry! As if huge numbers of people will gather to fight because of a meal or two! And even if Odysseus himself were to return, I don't think his wife would get much joy from seeing him die like a dog, defeated by superior numbers. But for now let us each go to our own house. The great Mentor and old Halitherses can deal with this journey idea."

So spoke Leiocritus, and the Assembly broke up, with each man going to his own house – apart from the suitors, who returned to the house of Odysseus.

Telemachus made his way down to the shore of the loud-resounding sea, where he washed his hands in the grey seawater. Then he raised them and prayed to Athena: "Oh lady, you came to me yesterday and told me to cross the sea to learn about my father. But the Achaeans hinder me – and the vile suitors most of all."

He looked around and there stood Athena disguised as Mentor.

"Telemachus," she said, "if you are truly the son of Odysseus and Penelope, you will prove to be a fine man. Ignore the suitors. They are reckless fools with no sense of what's right. Little do they know of the black fate that awaits them, when they shall die in a single day.

"As for your journey, you can depend on me as I'm an old friend of your father. I will fix up a ship for you. Go, now, to your house and join the suitors. Make provisions for the journey: wine in jars and barley in sacks. I will go through town and gather a crew. There are plenty of ships in the harbour, and I'll find you a good one. Then we'll sail over the wine-dark sea."

So spoke Athena. Telemachus hurried home, his heart troubled. He found the suitors flaying goats and butchering swine in the courtyard. Antinoüs came up to him laughing and grasped his hand, saying: "Telemachus, my boy,

you're an excellent speaker, and very brave, but don't let hatred invade your heart. Eat, drink and be merry with the rest of us. I'm sure the Achaeans will fix up a ship for you to go to Pylos to seek information about your father."

"Really, Antinoüs," said Telemachus, withdrawing his hand. "I can hardly relax as you help yourself shamelessly to my property! Haven't you been taking advantage of me since I was a child? Well, I am a child no more. I have learned much from the talk of others, and a new strength of spirit is swelling in my breast. I shall go to Pylos, even if I have to travel in another's ship."

The suitors, who were feasting and carousing, mocked Telemachus and jeered at him. One of the arrogant nobles would say to another, "For sure he's out to get us! Perhaps he will bring men from Pylos or Sparta! Or he means to harvest deadly drugs he can put in the wine bowl and kill us all!"

So spoke the suitors to one another. But Telemachus went down to his father's treasure chamber, a large room in which piles of gold and bronze stood along the wall, and where chests lay filled with clothes and jars of

fragrant oil. Jars of wine also stood against the wall, ready for Odysseus, should he come home. The doors to the chamber were closed and the old faithful slave, Eurycleia, who had nursed Telemachus as a child, sat on a chair in front of them. Day and night she protected the room.

"Nurse, draw me off some wine," Telemachus said, "not the best but the second best. The best is for my father, if he should come home, escaping death. Fill twelve jars with this wine and give me twenty measures of barley in leather sacks. Don't tell anybody! In the evening I'll come back to get these supplies, when my mother goes upstairs to her chamber. For I'm going to Sparta and sandy Pylos to see if I can find out anything about my father."

"Oh, my child!" Eurycleia shrieked in distress. "What made you think of this? You are an only child and much beloved, and your father has surely died in some strange land. As soon as you are gone these men will find new ways to ruin your house. They'll divide your possessions. They'll devise evil. Stay here, Telemachus, and mind your property. Please, do not go across the sea!"

"Dear nurse, don't worry," Telemachus said. "I'll be fine. The gods are involved. But swear that you will say nothing to my mother until the eleventh or twelfth day, or until she hears I am gone. I don't want her weeping all this time."

So he spoke, and Eurycleia swore a binding oath. Then she opened the doors and went into the room and filled twelve jars with wine and poured barley meal into sacks. Telemachus went back into the hall to join the suitors.

Meanwhile Athena, the shining goddess, put on the form of Telemachus and went through the city. Whenever she came to a loyal man, she'd say to him, "Go down to the harbour tonight." And from a man named Noemon, a sailor, she asked for a ship, and he said "Yes."

The sun set and the ways grew dark. Athena in the guise of Telemachus called for the ship to be moored near the entrance to the harbour. Around it gathered Ithacans eager for the journey.

Athena went to the house of Odysseus and cast a spell on the suitors, causing sleepiness to overcome them. Their minds wandered as they drank and their cups fell from their hands. They got up to go back to their own houses to sleep.

Athena, as Mentor, called Telemachus into the courtyard.

"Telemachus," she said, "companions await you down at the shore. Come, let us go!"

So saying, Athena led the way and Telemachus followed.

"Come, my friends, let's go up to the house," Telemachus said to the companions when he reached the shore, "and get the stores for our journey. No one knows of this, not even my mother. Only one of the handmaids whom I trust."

They collected the provisions and took them down to the boat and stowed them. Athena stepped into the vessel and sat at the back, with Telemachus beside her. The men let loose the stern cables and boarded, sitting down on benches. They set up the mast in a hollow socket in the middle of the boat, and made it fast with forestays. They raised a white sail and tied it with twisted thongs of ox hide. Athena sent a fair wind that whistled over the sea, and the gusts filled the belly of the sail. The dark waves sang about the prow as the crew sped on their way. They set out bowls brimming with wine and poured offerings to the gods and above all to flashing-eyed Athena, the daughter of Zeus. All night long they sailed through the dark until the sun began to rise.

Book 3

TELEMACHUS
MEETS NESTOR

The sun rose into the bronzed sky, bringing light to the divine gods and to mortals on the grain-giving earth. Telemachus and his crew came to the kingdom of Pylos, ruled by Nestor, one of the wisest of the men who went to Troy. On the shore were a large group preparing to sacrifice nine bulls to the dark-haired immortal god Poseidon, lord of the seas. The citizens of Pylos would burn the thigh pieces on the fire in the god's honour and eat the innards.

The ship pulled in to land. The Ithacans stowed the sail and stepped onto the sand. They secured the boat while Athena got out, with Telemachus following behind.

"Telemachus, you need no longer feel ill at ease," the goddess said, turning to him. "Not even the slightest amount. You've travelled across the sea to find out about your father. Go straight to King Nestor and ask him. He will tell you what he knows."

"But Mentor, I wouldn't know how to address him," said Telemachus. "How does a young man question an elder?"

"Just say what comes to mind. The gods will help you."

Athena led the way into the crowd of Pylians attending the sacrifice on the shore. They came to Nestor, sitting with his sons. Men were roasting meat on the nearby fire, but when they saw Telemachus and Athena disguised as Mentor they went up to them and greeted them warmly.

Nestor's son Pisistratus spread fleeces on the sand so they could sit near his father. Pisistratus served them roasted intestines and poured wine into a golden cup.

"Pray now to Poseidon, lord of the seas," Pisistratus said as he handed Athena the cup. "For you have come to his festival. When you have finished, pass the cup to your friend so that he too may offer libations. I have no doubt that he prays to the gods who rule all things. Because he is clearly the younger of the two of you, I give you the cup first."

Pisistratus placed in Athena's hand the cup of sweet wine. The goddess was delighted at his good manners, giving the cup first to her.

"Hear me, lord Poseidon, and grant us what we ask!" she said. "To Nestor and his sons give renown, and to the Pylians give good fortune. Grant that Telemachus and I accomplish our purpose."

So she prayed, even though it was Athena herself who was bringing all this to pass. She gave the beautiful cup with two handles to Telemachus and he prayed in the same way. Once the meat of the sacrifice was cooked, they removed it from the spits and placed it in a pile, then shared it out.

When they had satisfied their hunger and their thirst, Nestor said, "Now it seems the right moment for us to find out who you travellers are. Where do you come from? Have you sailed across the sea on business, or are you taking your chances, like evil pirates intent on wreaking havoc?"

"Nestor, son of Neleus, famous among the Achaeans, you ask where we come from and I will tell you," said Telemachus politely. "We're from the island of Ithaca. We do not come on public business; our interest is personal. We are here searching for news of my father, Odysseus, son of Laertes. I know that you fought with him in the war against Troy. We have heard about the terrible deaths of the warriors there, but we know nothing about how my father died – whether he was killed by enemies on the mainland or whether he drowned at sea. If ever Odysseus was of service to you in Troy, please tell me the truth."

"You remind me of terrible times and all that we suffered," Nestor replied, "and I think of the men who died at Troy, the best of the Achaeans. There now lies dead mighty Ajax, and the magnificent Achilles, and Patroclus, Achilles' friend – and my own son, Antilochus, a superb fighter. Yes, it would take a long time to tell you of the horrors we suffered. Even if you were to stay five years or six years and I spoke the whole time, telling you of the sorrows we bore on the plain of Troy, still you would leave without having heard them all.

"For nine long years we fought beneath the towering walls which Zeus would not allow to fall. Then thanks to the great cunning of your father – such a clever man! – we took the city.

"After we sacked the city we fell into further strife. The flashing-eyed goddess, Athena, daughter of Olympian Zeus, caused almighty trouble between Menelaüs and Agamemnon, the sons of Atreus. They called an assembly of the Achaeans, and we gathered as the sun set. The men were heavy with wine. The sons of Atreus explained that there were opposing views about the best plan of action. Menelaüs thought we should get to our ships and return home as soon as possible, but Agamemnon argued we should stay and perform a great sacrifice to thank the gods, especially Athena, who might cause us mishap on our return journey.

"We parted, each side thinking dark thoughts about the other. When morning came, half of us loaded our ships with booty, including women we had taken in the war, and launched on the sea. Half held back. When we in the ships got as far as the island of Tenedos, just off the coast, we stopped and offered sacrifices to the gods, begging for a swift return – but disputes broke out again and some turned back, including your father Odysseus. I went on, unsure whether to sail on the open seas past Chios or whether we should hug the coast, but the gods gave a sign and we sailed across open water as far as Euboea. There we paused to make a sacrifice to Poseidon. Then I sailed around the Peloponnesus here to Pylos. It took four days.

"So that's what happened, my child. I didn't hear about many of the homecomings, but I do know that the Myrmidons returned, Achilles' men. The great Philoctetes made it home to Thessaly, and Idomeneus got home to Crete; none of his men who survived the war were lost at sea. But have you already heard about what happened to Agamemnon, the son of Atreus? Aegisthus devised a shameful death for him. Fortunately, he left a son behind, Orestes, who took his revenge."

"Yes, Nestor, truly Orestes did take his revenge," Telemachus said. "I only wish the gods would give me strength like that. Then I could take revenge on the men courting my mother and destroying my property! But what can I do? I must endure."

"My friend, since you bring this up," said Nestor, "I have heard about the suitors who besiege you. Do you let them do this? Or do all the people hate you? Who knows, someday Odysseus may return and take vengeance, either by himself or maybe with his men. Ah, I wish that Athena might love you as she loved Odysseus in the land of Troy, where we suffered so much. For never have I seen the gods as interested in a man as Athena was in Odysseus. If she loved you as she loved him, then one or two of the suitors might regret their behaviour!"

"Sir, I'm sorry but I don't think this will ever happen," said Telemachus. "My father's return is so unlikely even the idea of it amazes me. No, this can never come to pass, not even if the gods want it."

"Telemachus! What are you saying?" whispered Athena, disappointed at his words. "A god can bring a man home, from no matter how far away. And I'd rather suffer every ill on a laborious journey home than return swiftly and be murdered immediately, the way Agamemnon was killed by Aegisthus and his treacherous wife Clytemnestra. The gods can never stop death, of course, when its time comes."

"Mentor, let's not talk about this," Telemachus answered. "My father can never come home. It's impossible. The gods have devised black death for him. But now I'd like to ask Nestor another question. He has ruled for three generations, so I'm told, and seems to know everything."

Telemachus turned to Nestor.

"So, Nestor, how did it come about that Aegisthus killed Agamemnon? Where was Menelaüs? And what kind of treachery did Aegisthus perform that enabled him to kill a far stronger man? Was Menelaüs not in Mycenae? Was he someplace else, meaning that Aegisthus took his chance?"

"Menelaüs and I set out together on our way back from Troy," Nestor replied, "but when we came to Sunium, the Cape of Athens, Apollo must have fired his arrows into Menelaüs' helmsman as he held the steering oar in his hand. So Menelaüs decided to stay at Sunium and bury the helmsman properly. When he set sail again, he came to the heights of Mallia, where he got caught up in a terrible storm. The waves were huge like mountains! The storm split the fleet, with some ships going to Crete, some to Egypt.

"Now, in Crete there's a high cliff off the coast where the wind drives waves against the headland. Some of the ships were destroyed there, though the men escaped. Five other ships sailed to Egypt where they gathered much wealth, including gold.

"It was during this time that Aegisthus killed Agamemnon. For seven years Aegisthus reigned over Mycenae – but in the eighth year Orestes, son of Agamemnon, reached manhood and killed him. Then Orestes held a big funeral feast for Aegisthus and for his hateful mother, Clytemnestra, whom he also killed! On that very day Menelaüs returned to Sparta, bringing ships loaded with treasure.

"So, my boy," Nestor continued, "take care not to stay too long away from your home, because those evil suitors may divide up all your possessions between them. Then your journey will have been for nothing. But first, I urge you – go to see Menelaüs in Sparta. He's returned from a land so far distant across the sea that it takes the birds who migrate there more than a whole year to cross such vast and terrible waters. But he is back home now. You can get there by land. I'll loan you a chariot and fine horses and Pisistratus will accompany you and show the way. You can ask Menelaüs to tell you the truth. He's a good man and I'm sure he will."

The sun went down and it was growing dark.

"King Nestor, this is good advice," said Athena. "But let us cut out the tongues of the cattle and throw them in the fire and pour offerings, begging Poseidon and the other gods for favour. Already the light has gone and it is time for sleep."

Slaves poured water over their hands and filled bowls with wine. They cut the tongues from the animals, threw them in the fire and poured wine on them. When Athena and Telemachus had finished and drunk their fill, they got up, eager to return to their ship.

"No, no, you must not go!" said Nestor, "As if we have nothing to offer you! I assure you we have plenty of soft blankets to sleep in comfort. Let no one say that I let the son of Odysseus sleep on the deck of a ship! Not so long as I live and my house prospers!"

"Well spoken, old friend," Athena said, "and I think that Telemachus should do as you say. This is better. Take Telemachus to your house. But I must return to the ship to see that all is well and tell the men what has happened. In the morning, I must visit a people up north, the Ciconians, because they owe me a large debt. But tomorrow morning send Telemachus on his way in a good chariot with strong horses and your son as a guide."

So saying, Athena turned into an eagle and flew away, to the astonishment of everyone.

"Young man!" said Nestor, amazed. "I don't think you will have any trouble proving your birth if at such a tender age you have gods looking out for you! I think that was Athena, the daughter of King Zeus, who watched over your father on the plain of Troy!"

Nestor took a cup and poured wine onto the ground, saying, "Dear goddess, bring us good fortune!"

After the offering they drank, then went to their own houses. Nestor led Telemachus to the airy portico where a corded bedstead was waiting. A bed for Pisistratus was set up beside him. Nestor himself slept in the innermost chamber of the house, and beside him slept his lovely wife.

When dawn came, Nestor got up and went out of his bed chamber through the house to the courtyard. There he sat on a polished throne and held a sceptre in his hands. Soon his sons and daughters arrived at the court, and Pisistratus with Telemachus.

"Come my children, help me," Nestor said. "We will have a feast. Bring out seats and logs for the fire, and bring in clear water too."

They got to work. The heifer came in from the plain and Telemachus' men arrived from the ships. The goldsmith came carrying his hammer and tongs to work the gold. Nestor gave chunks of gold to the smith who formed it into sheets and overlaid it on the horns of the heifer.

One son led the heifer by the horns into the centre. Another brought water in a basin decorated with little flowers. In his other hand he held a basket filled with barley grains. A third son held an axe. Nestor began the hand washing. He sprinkled barley grains over the head of the heifer, prayed to Athena, then cut hair from the heifer's head and threw it in the fire. Nestor's son brought down the axe, cutting through the sinews of the neck. The heifer's legs collapsed and the women cried out. Then men raised up the heifer's head and held it while Pisistratus cut its throat. Black blood flowed into a bowl and the animal died.

They cut up the body into pieces and took out the thigh pieces, which they covered with a double layer of fat and bits of meat. Nestor burned the thigh pieces on billets of wood as he poured sparkling wine over them. Beside him men stood with five-pronged forks. When the thigh pieces were wholly burned, and the men had tasted the inner parts of the heifer with their five-pronged forks, they roasted the cut-up meat on spits.

The meat was roasted and they ate it, constantly pouring wine into golden goblets. When they were satisfied, Nestor arose to speak.

"My sons, get ready a chariot for Telemachus. Prepare the finest horses you can find."

They obeyed and readied the chariot, yoking handsome horses. The house slave came out and packed inside bread and wine and other good things. Telemachus got in the chariot with Pisistratus beside him. Pisistratus took the reins and flicked a whip to start the horses. They sped down into the plain below Pylos and rode all day long.

The sun set and the way grew dark. They came to a house that Pisistratus knew. There they stayed for the night and were treated like kings.

When dawn appeared, they yoked the horses to the chariot, mounted and drove out of the echoing courtyard onto the plain. The horses ran before them. The sun set and the ways grew dark.

Book 4

TELEMACHUS IN SPARTA

Telemachus and Pisistratus came to hollow Lacedaemon, the land over which Sparta ruled, riven with many ravines, and they drove straight to the palace of King Menelaüs. He was in the midst of a marriage feast and all his relatives were there. It was a double feast for both his son, Megapenthes, and his daughter Hermionê. Menelaüs was sending Hermionê to marry Neoptolemus, the son of Achilles, making good his promise from when he was in Troy.

All the neighbours and kin of Menelaüs were feasting in the great high-roofed hall. In the corner a musician sang and played beautiful music with his lyre, while at the heart of the crowd two acrobats tumbled and bounded across the floor.

As Telemachus and Pisistratus drew up their chariot at the palace's outer gate, one of Menelaüs' men hastened to the King.

"King Menelaüs, divine in your origins, some noble men have come to the outer gates. Shall I see to their horses, or should I send them on their way?"

"Don't speak like a fool!" said Menelaüs angrily. "Many times on our journey home we were hosted at different houses. Unharness their horses of course, and invite these men to join us in our wedding feast!"

The attendant hastened through the hall, calling on others to help. They loosened the sweating horses and led Telemachus and Pisistratus into the palace.

Telemachus and Pisistratus went into the bathing area and slaves came in to wash them and anoint them with scented oil. The slaves put tunics on their shoulders and fleecy cloaks. Then Telemachus and Pisistratus went into the main hall and sat down on chairs near Menelaüs. A slave brought in water for their hands and poured it from a beautiful pitcher of gold over a silver basin. Other slaves drew up a polished table and set out bread and dainties. A carver brought platters of meats and set them down beside the goblets of gold.

"Please eat the food and celebrate!" Menelaüs said. "Once you've eaten you can tell us who you are."

When they had eaten their fill, Telemachus leaned into Pisistratus to talk privately.

"Pisistratus, look at the flashing of bronze and gold and silver and ivory in these halls!" he said. "This must be like the court of Zeus on Olympus. Untold wealth beyond anything I've ever seen!"

"My children, I'm afraid no mortal could compete with Zeus," Menelaüs said, overhearing Telemachus. "I suffered greatly bringing these treasures home in the eighth year after the war. I travelled far and wide, through Cyprus and Phoenicia, Egypt and Ethiopia, Sidon – and Libya, where the lambs are horned and give birth three times a year and everybody has enough meat and cheese and milk.

"While I was wandering in those distant lands an evil lowlife killed my brother Agamemnon, conspiring with his depraved wife Clytemnestra – so perhaps you will understand that I take no joy in this wealth. I'd rather own a fraction of what I possess but have all the men who died at Troy still live! I've often sat in my halls weeping for them until I could weep no longer.

"But there is one man I mourn more than any other . . . and that is Odysseus. He was the best, and thinking about him brings nothing but sorrow. He's been gone so long, and no one knows where he is – whether he's alive or dead. His father Laertes must mourn him, I'm sure, and his lovely wife Penelope too. Also, he had a little son when he left for Troy, named Telemachus. I wonder where he is now."

The mention of his father stirred deep sorrow in Telemachus and he began to weep. He raised his cloak to his eyes.

At that moment Helen emerged from her perfumed chamber. She was like Artemis in her beauty. Several slaves accompanied her. One set out a chair, beautifully inlaid, and another brought in a wool rug and placed it over the chair. A third carried in a silver basket that Helen had been given by an Egyptian lady in Thebes, when she and Menelaüs stayed there on their return from Troy.

"Menelaüs," Helen said, "do we know who these men are? Let me be honest. Never in my life have I seen anyone resemble another the way this man resembles Telemachus, son of Odysseus. He was just a baby when that great fighter sailed to Troy and you went looking for war – because of me and my callous ways."

"You know, my dear wife, I noticed the resemblance myself," said Menelaüs. "You see it in his hands, his eyes, his head, his hair . . . And just now I mentioned Odysseus, relating his troubles during the war, and tears fell from the young man's eyes."

"King Menelaüs," said Pisistratus, "this man is Telemachus, son of Odysseus. But he's prudent and he doesn't wish to burden you with his troubles unasked. Nestor, King of Pylos, your companion in war, sent me as his guide. Telemachus was eager to see you in case you might give him news of Odysseus. For a son has plenty of trouble to contend with when his father's gone and there are no others to help."

"I can't believe this!" burst out Menelaüs in wonder. "Can it be true, that the son of a man I loved so much – who suffered so much, for my sake – has come to my house! Why, I have always thought that if Odysseus ever came back I would welcome him above all others. I would give him a city to live in somewhere here under my rule – drive out the people there and build him a house. I'd bring him from Ithaca with all his possessions and his slaves, and we would often be together, until the black cloud of death finally enfolded us. But I suppose the gods had other plans, for they never gave this man a homecoming."

Menelaüs' words caused them all to weep.

"Menelaüs, son of Atreus, esteemed Nestor, my father, always told me you were the wisest man," Pisistratus said. "The shedding of all these tears makes me think of my brother who died at Troy. I never knew him but they say he was a fine fighter, Antilochus by name."

"Antilochus? A fine man!" agreed Menelaüs. "You seem to be wise, too, and know more than your age warrants. Lucky is he who has a good marriage and many children, the way your father Nestor does! He has reached a very old age and clearly his sons are intelligent and, I suppose, good fighters. But let us move on from all this crying now. I want to talk to Telemachus."

A slave poured water over his hands. They all looked forwards to the good cheer lying before them. The wine was mixed in a large bowl and, secretly, Helen added to the liquid a drug that would quiet all pain and bring forgetfulness of every ill. Helen had got these drugs from Polydamna when they were in Egypt, for the Egyptians have the best drugs, kinds that heal and kinds that kill.

"Menelaüs, my dear husband, whom Zeus loves so much," Helen said after they had drunk the wine, "and you other noble men, Zeus gives both good and evil. Enjoy this feast now and tell any stories you have. In fact I have a story to tell. I don't know about the marvellous feats that Odysseus accomplished in the war, but I do know one tale. This is what he did.

"One day, he marked his body as if he'd been beaten and put on a dirty cloak as if he were a stinking slave, then he infiltrated Troy looking like a beggar. He fooled everyone, but I saw right through the disguise. I questioned him, though he tried to avoid me. Then I gave him a bath and anointed his flesh with oil and put fresh clothes on him and I swore an oath not to tell the Trojans. Then after stabbing many Trojans, he slipped away and returned to your camp.

"The Trojan women whose husbands Odysseus had killed wailed with grief, but I paid no mind, for I had long before decided to return home to Sparta. I regretted the blindness that Aphrodite had cloaked me with, leading me to turn my back on my native land, my child, my wedding chamber and my precious husband."

"My dear, you have told that very well," Menelaüs observed. "I've travelled over the wide world and known many men, but never did I know a man like Odysseus. Another example of his fine work was when we were hiding inside the hollow horse, ready to kill the Trojans. Some god must have been behind your actions. You walked around the horse three times, touching it with your hands and calling out in all the different voices of the wives of all the men inside the horse. I was crouching with Diomedes and I was tempted to cry out when I heard you, and so was Diomedes, but Odysseus stopped us betraying ourselves. That made the other Achaeans keep quiet, too, except for Anticlus. He wanted to answer, but great Odysseus put a hand over his mouth and saved us. I suppose it was Athena who led you away, at last."

"And yet, King Menelaüs, leader of your people," said Telemachus, "all Odysseus' goodness and strength did him no good. Forgive me. We are tired and in sore need of sleep."

Helen told her slaves to set up bedsteads beneath the portico and dress them with beautiful purple blankets and covers. That was where Telemachus and Pisistratus, the son of Nestor, slept, in the porch of the palace. Menelaüs, the son of Atreus, slept in an inner chamber, and beside him lay beautiful Helen, a wonder among women.

At dawn Menelaüs rose from his bed and put on his clothes. He cast around his shoulders a strap that held his sword. He tied on his sandals and went out into the court to find Telemachus sitting there.

"Telemachus, tell me *why* have you come over the dark sea?" Menelaüs asked abruptly. "Is it on some public matter or is it private?"

"Menelaüs, commander of men," Telemachus answered, "I have come hoping you might tell me something about my father. My household is being ravaged and my lands are ruined and my home is filled with evil men who slaughter my sheep and cattle – 'suitors' of my mother, so they claim, insolent to the core. So I am here in the hope, Menelaüs, that you might tell me of my father's sad death, whether you saw it with your own eyes or heard about it from somebody else. Do not take pity on me and say soothing words, but tell me the reality of it. If ever my father was a friend to you in the land of Troy, I pray you – tell me the truth!"

Menelaüs was indignant at what Telemachus related. "To Hades' house with those people! What cowards they are! Just as when a doe gives birth in a lion's lair, then roams over the valleys looking for pasture, and then the lion comes back – what do you imagine happens to the fawns? Let Odysseus pour death on these suitors! I remember a time when he wrestled a man on the island of Lesbos and threw him down so violently that all the Achaeans shouted for joy. Even so will these men discover his power and meet an early death. As for your father, I'll tell you everything I heard from Proteus, the Old Man of the Sea.

"I was stuck in Egypt. The gods were angry because I failed to make the proper offerings, something you should never fail in. Now, there's an island in front of Egypt called Pharos. It's about as far as a ship runs in a whole day when a good wind is blowing. It has a harbour to anchor in while drawing water. Well, there the gods held me for twenty days, and the winds never blew in the right direction. My stores would soon be gone and my men's strength ruined – if a god had not saved me: Eidothea, the daughter of Proteus, the Old Man of the Sea.

"Eidothea met me as I wandered along the shore while my comrades fished around the island because they were starving. She came up and said, 'Are you such a fool, stranger, that you stay of your own will here on this island?' I replied, 'I don't know which goddess you are, but I assure you I'm not stuck here willingly. I must have upset the gods, but can you tell me how I can get going again?'

"'Since you ask, stranger, I'll tell you everything,' she said. 'Every day Proteus of Egypt comes here, the Old Man of the Sea. He serves Poseidon. They say he is my father. If you lie in wait and catch him he will tell you how you can get back. He will also tell you what good and what evil has been done at home while you've been away.'

"'But how can I lie in wait for the Old Man and not be seen? It's hardly easy to fool a god!' I said.

"'At noon the Old Man comes out of the sea, when West Wind ripples the surface. He lies down to sleep in caves and seals gather around him, the brood of the Daughter of the Sea. The smell is foul! I will lead you to the caves at daybreak. Choose three men as companions. I will lay you in the right places.

"'Be warned that the Old Man is filled with magic. First, he will count the seals. When he has counted them off by fives, he lies down like a shepherd with his flock and falls asleep. As soon as you see him lying down, you must hold him down, no matter how hard he resists. He will change into all kinds of earthly things and even into blazing fire. Still, hold him and don't let go until he appears in his original form. Then release him and ask him who of the gods is so angry with you.'

"Then Eidothea dived into the sea. I went to my ships, pondering many dark things. We prepared our dinner and the night fell. We lay down to rest on the beach. At dawn I walked along the shore, praying to the gods and taking with me the three comrades I trusted most.

"In the meantime, Eidothea had come back with four sealskins, freshly flayed. She scooped out four troughs in the sand. She made us lie down in the troughs and placed a sealskin over each of us. The foul smell of the skins was so great that we couldn't stand it and the plan was nearly ruined. Then Eidothea brought in a perfume and placed it beneath our noses.

"We waited all morning. Finally the seals came out and lay down in rows along the shore. The Old Man of the Sea came out of the waves and counted the fat seals, starting with us but never guessing we were there. Then he lay down and we jumped up and grabbed him. He turned into a lion, then a snake, then a leopard, then a gigantic boar, then flowing water, then he became a tall tree covered with leaves. But we held on. At last he grew tired and returned to his original form.

"'Who are you?' he asked. 'Why have you held me against my will?'

"'Old Man of the Sea,' I answered, 'you know how long I've been held on this island and, in truth, my will is weakening. Tell me – which god is preventing my return?'

"'If you had made proper offerings to Zeus and the other gods, you would have had better fortune,' Proteus said. 'As it is, you must now go back to Egypt and the beautiful Nile river and make sacrifices there. Only once you have done this can you find your way home.'

"I was stunned to hear him say that once again I would have to journey across the sea to Egypt.

"'Alright I will, Old Man. But tell me, did all the captains return unharmed from Troy?'

"'O son of Atreus, Menelaüs, for that is who I think you are,' Proteus said, 'why do you question me about this? You will only be reduced to

tears. Many men were killed on the windy plain, as you know, but two perished on their homeward journey and there is a third, I think, still held somewhere.

"'The lesser Ajax was lost at sea. As you know, his namesake, the greater Ajax, died at Troy from madness and shame. At first Poseidon drove the lesser Ajax's long-oared ships against the rocks on the south coast of Mykonos. But Ajax was saved, even though Athena hated him because he raped Cassandra, Priam's daughter, at the base of the goddess' own statue in Troy. Then lesser Ajax, the blind fool, shouted from a rock that, in spite of the gods, he had escaped the sea. Poseidon heard him and took up his trident to shatter the rock. Ajax was driven deep into the cold water and there he died.

"'As for your brother, Agamemnon, Hera smiled on him – at first. A storm caught him off Malia, at the tip of the Peloponnesus, and carried him a good way, but then the wind blew fair. He got home to Mycenae. Coming off the boat he kissed the land and tears streamed from his eyes. Aegisthus controlled Mycenae at this time. He chose twenty of his best men and set them to lie in wait. He prepared a great feast, then went in his chariot to meet Agamemnon, brought him to the house, and when he had entertained him, he killed him like an ox at the corn crib. He killed his retainers too, and then he killed his own followers so that no one would know what happened.'

"This is what Proteus told me, and I was broken-hearted and I sank down on the sands. I no longer wished to live. But when I was spent from weeping, the Old Man of the Sea said:

"'Menelaüs, long grieving does you no good. Put your sorrow aside and get home as soon as you can. Perhaps you will find Aegisthus still alive, unless Orestes, the son of Agamemnon, has killed him.'

"'So much for the two names you mentioned, Ajax and Agamemnon," I said. "But who is the third man?'

"'Odysseus, the son of Laertes,' Proteus said, 'who lives on Ithaca. I saw him on an island, weeping in the house of the nymph Calypso, who keeps him against his will. He cannot return to his native land for he has no ships and no comrades to speed him on his way.

"'As for you, Menelaüs, you will not die in Sparta, but the gods will carry you to the Elysian Fields at the ends of the earth. Rhadamanthus dwells there, judge of the other world, and life is easy – there is no snow, storms or rain; Ocean sends up the kind West Wind that cools men. And you will have Helen for a wife.'"

"Then the Old Man of the Sea plunged beneath the surging waves. Back again we went to Egypt and the Nile river, and I moored my ships and offered huge offerings to the gods. Then I heaped up a burial mound to my brother Agamemnon so that his name may last forever.

"But come, Telemachus, stay here for eleven or twelve days and then I will send you forth with fine gifts – three horses, a sturdy chariot and a beautiful cup from which you can pour offerings to the immortal gods."

"Son of Atreus, you must not keep me here for a long time," said Telemachus, "although I would happily spend a year listening to your tales. Even at this moment my comrades await me in Pylos. And if you want to give a gift, make it a treasure that I can carry. I cannot take horses to Ithaca! In Ithaca there are no wide open spaces, no meadows at all. It is a land fit only for goats, but pretty."

"You speak well, my child," said Menelaüs, smiling. "Well, I will change the gift then. I will give you instead the most beautiful treasure I have: a mixing bowl of silver with rims of gold."

Meanwhile, back in Ithaca at the court of Odysseus, the suitors were playing idle games. One of the men, Noemon, addressed Antinoüs, one of the leaders. "Do we know when Telemachus is returning from Pylos?" he asked. "He left with a ship of mine and I need it to cross over to Ellis where I have broodmares and young mules."

The suitors were amazed because they thought that Telemachus had not gone to Pylos but was out on the land among the flocks, or with the swineherd Eumaeus.

"Tell me the truth, Noemon," Antinoüs said. "When did he go? Who went with him? Were they good men of Ithaca or hired men and slaves? Did he take your boat by force or did you give it to him willingly?"

"I gave it freely. What else could you do when a man like that, burdened with sorrow, asks you for something? And the men who went with him are the best. One of them was Mentor."

Antinoüs and Eurymachus were deeply angered and at once made the suitors stop their games. Antinoüs spoke to them in a rage, his black heart filled with fury.

"We imagined that Telemachus would never bring off this journey, but he has! He will bring us trouble! May Zeus destroy him before he reaches full manhood. Give me a swift ship and twenty men and I will ambush him in the strait between Ithaca and Cephalonia!"

Everyone praised his words and approved the plan.

The slave Medon heard the suitors plotting as he stood outside the court. He went up the stairs to Penelope's chamber.

"Medon, have the suitors sent you here?" Penelope asked as he stepped over the threshold. "What, will they have Odysseus' slaves prepare another feast? May this meal be their last! They come in a throng and squander the wealth of Telemachus. Surely their fathers told them the kind of man Odysseus was, that he never wronged anyone? He never dealt unjustly, but they are men without gratitude."

"Yes," Medon said, "but I wish this were the worst of all their faults. The suitors are planning a greater crime. They want to kill Telemachus as he sails home from Pylos and Sparta."

At his words, Penelope's knees trembled and a pain shot through her heart.

"Medon, why is my son gone?" she responded at last. "He didn't need to board a ship and cross the sea!"

"I don't know whether some god drove him on," Medon answered, "or whether it was his own idea. He wanted to go to Pylos to discover news of his father."

A cloud of grief fell on Penelope. All about her, her handmaids sobbed.

"Listen to me, my friends," she said finally. "No one has ever lived with more sorrow than I do. Long ago I lost my husband, and now my son is gone, swept away by the winds.

"Now summon Dolius who tends the trees in my garden. I want him to go to Laertes, Odysseus' father. Perhaps Laertes can plead with the people to resist these men bent on destroying his family!"

"Bride of Odysseus," said Eurycleia, the aged and loyal nurse among the handmaids, "I'll tell you no lie. I did know about this, and I gave Telemachus bread and wine for his journey. But he made me swear that I would not say a word until the twelfth day, so that you might not spoil your face with weeping. For now, take a bath and dress in fresh clothing and then pray to Athena to save Telemachus' life. And do not trouble old Laertes."

Eurycleia's words made Penelope feel a little better. She went to the bathroom, took a bath, put on clean clothing and went back to her upper chamber. She put barley grains in a basket and prayed to Athena.

"Hear me, Athena, child of Zeus," she said. "If ever Odysseus burned for you fat thighs in sacrifice, save my son. Ward off the evil suitors who plan to kill him!"

She cried out in prayer, and Athena did hear her.

Meanwhile, down in the hall, the suitors broke into uproar. "I suppose that the queen is getting our marriage ready, little knowing that death awaits her son!" said one to another.

"Let us not boast." Antinoüs addressed the company. "Someone may

overhear you. Let us get up now and put our plans into effect."

Antinoüs chose twenty men. They went down to the shore and drew a ship into the water. They stood up the mast and sail and fitted oars then spread the sail. Assistants brought them their weapons. Far out in the channel they moored the ship, before going ashore, preparing dinner and awaiting darkness.

Penelope lay in her upper chamber. She would not touch food, neither meat nor drink, and thought constantly about her son and whether he would escape death. She felt like a lion that is filled with terror when armed men surround him. Finally, sleep overcame her.

Athena created a phantom in the form of a woman and sent it into the house. The phantom passed through the seal of the chamber and stood at Penelope's head.

"Are you sleeping, Penelope, troubled at heart?" the phantom asked. "The gods do not want you to weep because your son has not returned. They hold nothing against him."

"Why have you come here?" Penelope responded. "You ask me to give up my grief and the pains that destroy me. It's been so long since I lost my husband, and now my son has gone away. He's just a child. He knows nothing of the world or the gatherings of men."

"Don't be afraid," the phantom said. "A guide goes with him, Athena herself, and she takes pity on you and your sorrow. It is she who has sent me."

"If you are a god, come tell me, I beg of you! Does that man, my husband, still live, or is he in the House of Hades?"

"I shall not speak of him," the phantom answered. "It is wrong to speak words that are empty as the wind."

So saying the phantom glided away. Penelope woke up, her heart racing.

Meanwhile, the suitors in the channel got back in their boat. There is a rocky island between Ithaca and Cephalonia, not large but with a harbour. There they lay in wait for the son of Odysseus.

Book 5

ODYSSEUS ESCAPES

The goddess Dawn rose from her couch to bring light to the gods and to mortals. As she did so, the gods sat down in council, led by most powerful Zeus. Athena was recounting the sufferings of Odysseus, in thrall to the nymph Calypso.

"Father Zeus, and all of you who will never die," she began, "never after this time will a king be kind, gentle and righteous. He may as well be harsh and deal unjustly with his people! For none of you remembers the goodness of Odysseus, who cared for his subjects like a father. He lies in Calypso's halls, where she keeps him against his will. He cannot return to his own land – and now his wife's suitors intend to kill his son."

"My fair child, what are you saying?" Zeus replied. "Didn't you intend that Odysseus should return and take his revenge? As for Telemachus, help him reach his native land! You have the power.

"Hermes, my trusted messenger," he continued, "tell the nymph Calypso that we have decided that Odysseus shall go home. After many trials, he will reach the Phaeacians, a people close to us. The Phaeacians will honour him and give him bronze and gold and clothing, more than he would have taken from Troy. This summer he is fated to see his people again."

Hermes bound golden sandals beneath his immortal feet and sailed like the wind over the sea and the vast land. He took his wand that can bring sleep over people's eyes and rouse them from slumber, too. In Thessaly, he dropped down into the sea like a cormorant hunting fish, its thick feathers in the water, and sped through the waves.

Hermes came to a great cave, the dwelling place of beautiful Calypso. Inside, a large fire burned on the hearth. The scent of burning cedar spread over the island and Calypso sang with a sweet voice as she went back and forth before her loom, weaving with a golden shuttle. The cave was nestled within a luxuriant wood of birch, poplar and cypress where birds made their nests: owls, falcons and chattering crows. Beside the cave was a garden of vines from which clusters of grapes dangled. Four springs in a row flowed with bright water. All around stood meadows where violets and celery bloomed.

Calypso invited Hermes to sit. "Hermes, my beloved friend whom I never see . . . Welcome! Why have you come? But before you answer, why don't you have something to eat?"

She placed before him ambrosia and nectar, food of the gods.

"You ask me what I've come for," Hermes said when he had finished dining, "and I will tell you. Zeus sent me here. He says that a man is here with you, a man more wretched than all who fought around Priam's city for nine years and in the tenth sacked it and went home. The rest of his men died, but the waves carried him here. Zeus bids you send him on his way because it is not his fate to die far from his native land."

"You gods are cruel and quick to envy!" Calypso said in sudden anger. "When Dawn took the hunter Orion to her bed, Artemis cut him down in a shower of golden arrows. And when Demeter slept with Iasion in the thrice-ploughed field, Zeus struck Iasion with his thunderbolt. In the same way, you are envious that a mortal man is my companion. I saved him when he rode the waves clutching a broken keel, all alone after Zeus shattered his ship. The rest of his men died but the sea brought him here. I welcomed him and gave him food and said I would make him immortal. But if Zeus wants this, there is nothing to be done. I have no ships and men for him to sail with, but I will advise him."

"Good!" said Hermes. "Send him forth so that you do not arouse the anger of Zeus."

Hermes left and Calypso went to Odysseus. She found him on the shore, his eyes wet with sadness and his life ebbing away as he grieved.

"Dear unhappy man," Calypso said, "you don't need to sorrow anymore. I am happy to send you on your way. Let us cut down timbers and make a raft and fasten planks for a deck. I'll load it with bread and water and wine to keep hunger away, and I will give you clothes. I will send a fair wind so that you may return unharmed to your native land. Such is the will of the gods who hold heaven, and they are more powerful than I."

"I think you're planning something else, goddess!" said Odysseus, shuddering. "You want me to cross the huge gulf of a sea, which not even ships pass over, just on planks? I will set foot on no raft, goddess, unless you swear that you are not plotting and devising some new mischief."

"You are a rascal, and so clever that you should think of such a thing," said Calypso, smiling and stroking his hand. "May the Earth be a witness, and the broad Sky, and the waters of Styx – the solemnest oath a god can make: I will not plot against you or cause you pain. My intentions are good, Odysseus."

So saying, the goddess led the way to her hollow cave, and Odysseus sat down on the chair Hermes had vacated. Calypso gave him food to eat and drink, and they enjoyed their meal. Calypso was first to speak.

"Son of Laertes, you are a clever man . . . are you sure you want to go home? If you really do, I wish you well. If you only knew the sufferings you will endure before you come to your land, you would stay here with me and live forever. I know you want to see your wife, but I'm not inferior in looks – we gods are better looking than humans!"

"Great goddess, don't be angry with me. I know that Penelope's not as radiant as you. She's a mortal after all, whereas you will live forever. Even so, I yearn for her day and night, and I want to go home. And if some god should strike me while I'm on the sea, I will endure it. I've suffered so much before, on the sea and in war. This will just be one more trouble."

Sunset and darkness came. They went into the innermost recess of her cave where they slept side by side.

The next morning, Odysseus dressed in a tunic and a cloak while the beautiful nymph put on a long white robe and tied around her waist a girdle of woven strands of gold. On her head she placed a scarf, then she set herself to aiding Odysseus' departure. She gave him a huge axe of bronze, sharpened on both sides, well fitted to his hands. The handle was olive and securely fastened to the head. She led the way to the edge of the island where tall trees grew, birch and cottonwood and fir, so large they reached the sky. The trees were dry and well seasoned, good for a raft.

After Calypso had shown Odysseus the trees, she returned to her cave. Odysseus swung into action, cutting the timber, working rapidly. He felled twenty trees and trimmed them, smoothed them and made them true. Meanwhile, Calypso returned, bringing drilling tools. Odysseus bored the planks and fitted them together and fixed them with pegs. The raft was as wide as a regular ship. He set up a mast and crossbar and made a steering oar. Calypso brought cloth for a sail.

On the fourth day, Odysseus had finished. On the fifth day, Calypso gave him a bath, dressed him in fragrant cloth and sent him on his journey. On the raft the goddess placed skins of wine and water, and provisions in a bag. Then she sent a fair wind, gentle and warm, to speed him on his way.

Gladly Odysseus spread his sails, guiding his raft skilfully with the steering oar. He did not sleep. He watched the stars as Calypso had advised him. He sailed for seventeen days, and on the eighteenth he saw the shadowy mountains of the land of the Phaeacians, like a shield lying on the misty sea.

Poseidon was coming back from his visit to the Ethiopians, and he saw Odysseus and became even angrier than he already was – because Odysseus had blinded his son, Polyphemus.

"A curse upon it!" Poseidon said to himself, shaking his head.

"I suppose the gods changed their mind about Odysseus while I was dining with the Ethiopians! He is near to the land of the Phaeacians, where he will escape his trials. All the same, I shall give him a little taste of evil!"

He gathered the clouds and, taking his trident, he roused every blast of every kind of wind. He covered the land with clouds, and night came rushing down. Odysseus' knees trembled and he was profoundly shaken.

"It looks like the end for me," he said to himself. "Everything the goddess said was true. Zeus has overcast the heaven and stirred up the sea. Destruction is sure. Three and four times blessed were those who died at Troy. I wish I had died when the Trojan gangs hurled their spears as we fought over the body of Achilles. I would have had a good funeral and the Achaeans would have spread my fame. But it seems I'm about to die a miserable death."

Even as he spoke, a wave struck him with terrible force, spinning his raft in a circle. He let go of the steering oar and tumbled into the sea. The mast broke in the middle and the crossbar fell. Odysseus was held under water, weighed down by the clothes that Calypso had given him.

Finally, he surfaced and spat out bitter brine. He lunged out to the raft and laid hold of it then pulled himself up on it and sat down in the middle, seeking to escape death. The seas bore the raft every which way. Just as in the autumn, North Wind carries the tufts of thistles over the plain, and they cling close to one another, even so did the winds toss the raft this way and that.

But Ino, once the mortal daughter of Cadmus, King of Thebes, saw him. Ino, she of the beautiful ankles, was now the White Goddess, a goddess in the deep sea. She pitied Odysseus when she saw him in trouble, and she came out of the waters like a seagull and sat on the raft.

"Miserable man, why does Poseidon hate you so?" Ino asked. "For all his anger, he will not kill you. Get rid of your clothes and swim to the land of the Phaeacians where you will escape. Come, take this cloth and tie it across your chest. It is divine and you will never be harmed while you are

wearing it. But once you get to land, untie the cloth and throw it into the sea, then turn away."

The goddess gave him the cloth and plunged into the water where the dark waves hid her.

Troubled, Odysseus muttered to himself, "I hope that one of the gods is not again trapping me. I will not obey. The land is far away. So long as the timbers hold, I'll tough it out – but when the raft shatters I will swim. No other choice!"

Poseidon sent a great wave – huge, terrifying! – that arched from up above and drove its full force down on him. Just as a strong wind tosses a dried-out heap of straw, casting some here and some there, so the wave scattered the pieces of the raft.

Odysseus clambered onto a single plank as if he were riding a horse and he stripped off his clothes. He stretched Ino's cloth across his chest and threw himself off the plank into the sea, his hands outstretched, ready to swim.

For two nights and two days Odysseus was driven over the waves. Many times, he thought he'd had it, but at dawn on the third day the wind dropped and calmness fell. He glimpsed the shore close at hand just as he was raised up by an enormous wave – and the sight of the land was like

the sight of his beloved children would be for a man who had been sick to death and then come back to life.

When Odysseus was as far away from shore as a man's voice carries when shouted, he heard the boom of the sea on the rocks. The waves thundered against the dry land, belching on it, wrapping everything in foam. For there were no harbours here, only headlands and cliffs.

"Zeus grants me sight of land, but I see no way out of the sea! There are only sharp crags and the waves' foaming roar. The cliffs run up sheer and the water is deep even close to land, so I can never stand up. If I try to get ashore a big wave may smash me against the rock. If I swim on to find a beach or harbour, the storm winds may catch me again and carry me out to sea. Or some god may even send a monster. I know how Poseidon wants to do me harm!"

As Odysseus debated in his mind, a huge wave crashed him against the shoreline. All his skin would have been stripped away and his bones broken if he had not seized the rock with both hands and clung to it, groaning, until the wave passed. But the undertow came in again and struck him and flung him into the sea. Just as when an octopus is dragged from its hole, and clean pebbles cling to its suckers, so bits of skin were stripped from Odysseus' hands onto the rocks.

Fighting his way out of the breakers, Odysseus swam looking constantly towards land, hoping for a beach. He came to the mouth of a river, where there were no crags and there was shelter.

"Hear me, King, whoever you are!" he prayed to the river god. "I ask for help! The gods care for wanderers, and I have come to your stream after much suffering. Pity me!"

The river god stopped his current and spread calm. Odysseus climbed ashore and his knees gave way and he fell on his hands. His flesh was swollen and brine came out in streams from his mouth and nostrils. He lay hardly breathing, unable to speak, with barely strength to move because of the enormous tiredness that overcame him.

After a while, he revived, and his spirits returned. Odysseus took the cloth from around his chest and threw it into the river. A powerful wave carried it downstream and Ino, the White Goddess, received it. Odysseus left the river and sat down in the reeds, kissing the earth, the giver of grain. He was thoroughly shaken.

"What will happen to me? What will be the end? If I lie in the riverbed overnight, the frost may overcome me, and the breeze will be cool from the river in the early morning. If I climb up to the woods and lie down in the bushes, the cold might leave me but I will be prey to wild animals."

Still, the woods seemed the better choice. He found a spot next to a clearing. He crawled beneath two bushes which grew from the same root. The wind could never penetrate them, nor the sun's rays; nor could the rain drip through. Without delay, Odysseus swept together a bed of fallen leaves and he lay down in the middle and heaped leaves over himself. As a man hides a spark beneath embers in a remote farm, away from neighbours, and in doing so saves the seed of fire so that it won't need to be rekindled in the morning – so Odysseus covered himself with leaves. And Athena shed sleep on his eyes in order that he might recover from his fatigue.

Book 6

NAUSICAA

Odysseus lay sleeping, fully overcome with exhaustion. Meanwhile, Athena went to the city of the Phaeacians. In olden times, the Phaeacians lived in a land near the Cyclopes, but these supercilious beings who were stronger than them plundered them constantly. So their king, god-like Nausithous, led them to the island of Scheria, far away from the rest of humankind. He built a wall around the city there and constructed houses and temples for the gods, and he divided up the land for agriculture. When he died, his son Alcinoüs became king.

Athena went into the elegant bedchamber of Nausicaa and her two handmaids. The young princess was sleeping, as beautiful as a goddess. Taking on the form of one of her friends, Athena said:

"Nausicaa, why so careless? Your beautiful clothes are lying around crumpled and dirty, yet your time for marriage is not far away. So let's go to wash your clothes at the break of day. Urge your father to prepare mules and a wagon, because the washing place is a long distance from the city."

Dawn came, and Nausicaa went through the house to her father and mother. Her mother was sitting by the fireplace with handmaids, spinning yarn, and her father was on his way out to meet with the heads of the council. She came up close to her father.

"Daddy, won't you prepare for me a wagon with strong wheels so that I can take my soiled clothes to the river for washing?"

"Well, the mules don't mind, my child," he said, "and neither do I, so

take them! Go! The slaves will prepare a wagon for you, one with strong wheels and a high box."

He called the slaves and they made ready the wagon, leading up mules and yoking them to it. Nausicaa brought the clothes from her room and put them inside. Her mother filled a little chest with delicacies and poured wine into a skin. Nausicaa took the whip and reins and struck the mules. They clattered as they sped on.

They came to the streams of the river where the washing pools were. Torrents of water welled up from below and flowed over the stone with the strength to cleanse even the dirtiest of garments. They unhitched the mules and drove them along the river to graze on the sweet grass, then carried the clothes into the dark water. They trampled on them in the pools, making merry in rivalry with one another.

When the clothes were washed and all stains gone, they spread them in rows on the seashore where the dashing waves had washed the pebbles clean. They enjoyed a meal on the riverbank while waiting for the clothes to dry in the sun.

When they had finished eating, Nausicaa and her handmaids threw off their headgear to play a game of ball. Nausicaa led them all in song as they played. She stood out among her lovely handmaidens in beauty, just like the goddess Artemis, who roamed the mountains in pursuit of boar and deer and nymphs of the woods and stood out among Zeus' daughters.

Nausicaa tossed the ball, but her handmaids missed it and the ball disappeared into the water in a deep eddy. All the girls squealed and Odysseus awoke. He sat up and wondered what was going on.

"Where have I come?" he thought. "Are there people here who are cruel? Or do they like strangers, respecting the gods? I heard a cry like a maiden's cry, perhaps nymphs who wander the mountains. Have I come to a place of human speech? Let me look . . ."

Odysseus emerged from the bushes. He broke a leafy branch from the brush to cover his private parts. Like a mountain lion trusting in his strength, though beaten up by rain and the winds, eyes blazing, entering the sheepfold, driven by hunger – just so, Odysseus was about to enter the company of lovely girls, even though he was stark naked.

He was terrible to see, all crusted in salt, and the handmaids fled in terror. Only Alcinoüs' daughter held her ground. She faced Odysseus, and he didn't know whether to clasp her knees and offer up a prayer, or stay apart and use only his words. He thought it better to keep his distance, afraid that the girl might be offended if he clasped her knees.

"I clasp your knees, my queen . . . " he said. "Are you a goddess or a mortal? If you are a goddess you look most like Artemis, but if you are mortal, three times blessed are your father and mother and your brothers. They must feel joy when they see you dancing like a flower. That man is blessed above others who will one day lead you to his home. I've never seen a mortal like you, man or woman. In Delos I did see the shoot of a palm that sprang up beside Apollo's altar. I was there with many men who followed me on a journey that brought us terrible pain. I marvelled when I saw that palm, for I've never seen a tree spring from the earth like that – and in the same way I'm amazed to see you and afraid to touch your knees.

"But hard is the trouble I have had. Yesterday, on the twentieth day of my journey, I escaped from the sea. All that time the waves and winds carried me from the island of Ogygia, over which Calypso reigns. And now I come ashore, afraid to suffer some ill. The gods will bring me even more troubles. Queen, have pity. Show me the way to the city and give me a rag to cover me."

"Stranger, you don't seem a bad man," Nausicaa replied. "I will show you to the city and I'll tell you the name of this people. These are the Phaeacians who live here. I'm the daughter of Alcinoüs, the king, who possesses power among the Phaeacians."

Cupping her mouth, she called to her handmaidens.

"Stop! Where are you going at the sight of this man? He's no enemy! No enemy to the Phaeacians could come here – we are far away over the sea, and besides, the gods love us. No mortals have dealing with us. This is some wanderer who has come here and we must take care of him because strangers and beggars are from Zeus. Even a small gift will help him. Come, my friends, give the stranger food and drink, and give him a bath in the river where there is shelter."

The girls stopped and called to each other. They led Odysseus to a sheltered place, as Nausicaa suggested, and next to him they placed a tunic and cloak, and they gave him the olive oil in a golden flask.

"Girls, please stand away," Odysseus said, "so that I may wash the brine from my shoulders and rub my flesh with oil. I will not bathe in your presence. I am ashamed to be naked in your midst."

The girls stood at a distance. Odysseus washed himself in the river, removing the brine from his back and shoulders and head. When he'd washed and rubbed himself with oil, he put on the clothes that the girls had given him. Athena made him taller and stronger, and from his head his locks flowed in curls like a hyacinth flower. The goddess showered attractiveness on Odysseus' head and shoulders, the way a craftsman trained by Hephaestus would cover silver with gold.

Odysseus went by himself to sit down on the shore, shining in his beauty, and the girls were amazed to see him.

"Listen, girls, to what I'm about to say," Nausicaa said. "This man does not come to us without the gods' will! Before he seemed rough, but now he is like a god! I wish that such a man might someday be my husband and live here with me. But come, my friends, give the stranger food and drink!"

They quickly set food and drink before Odysseus and he ate ravenously.

In the meanwhile, Nausicaa folded the clothes and put them in the wagon. She yoked the mules and got in.

"Prepare yourself now, stranger, to go to the city," she called to Odysseus, "where I may show you the way to my father's house. There you will come to know the noblest Phaeacians. We will come to the city, which is inside a high wall. There's a harbour on either side and the causeway is narrow between the two harbours. Ships are drawn up on the sand there. Nearby is the place of assembly, beside the temple of Poseidon, marked by big stones in the earth. The men are busy with ships' tackle, with cables and sails and oar blades. The Phaeacians are not hunters, and they don't care for bows and quivers but for masts and oars and above all the ships. They rejoice to sail over the seas!

"But I am afraid of evil chatter. Some commoner might say, 'Well, who is this fellow with Nausicaa? Handsome and a stranger? Where did she find him? I suppose she's going to marry him.' That's what they'll say, and this would be a reproach to me.

"Stranger, do what I say. You will find a grove of Athena close to the road, up ahead. It's a grove of birch trees. Inside the grove are a spring and a meadow. That's my father's estate and vineyard, shouting distance from the city. Sit down in the grove and wait until we reach my father's house. When you think we must have arrived, go into the city and ask for the house of my father. It's easy to find. Even a child could show you the way.

"When you reach the house, walk right through the great hall until you come to my mother. She will be sitting by the fire spinning her yarn and leaning against a pillar while her handmaids sit around her. There, too, leaning against the same pillar, is my father's chair where he sits and drinks his wine. Walk past him and throw your arms around my mother's knees. Then you may see the day of your return, though you come from very far."

She lashed the mules with the whip and left the stream. Her handmaids and Odysseus followed on foot. The sun set. They came to the grove and Odysseus sat down and prayed.

"Hear me, O Athena! Listen to my prayer! Before this you did not listen when Poseidon wrecked me. Grant that I go to the Phaeacians as one to be pitied!"

Athena did hear him, but she did not appear in person, for she respected Zeus' brother, Poseidon, who raged against Odysseus until he reached his native land.

Book 7

IN THE COURT OF
THE PHAEACIANS

Odysseus prayed while the mules carried Nausicaa into the city. She came to the glorious palace of her father and stopped at the outer gate. Her handsome brothers rushed to help her unhitch the mules and carry the clothing inside. Nausicaa went to her own chamber.

Odysseus got up to walk into the city. Athena poured a mist around him so none of the Phaeacians might challenge him. When he was about to enter the city walls, Athena met him, disguised as a young girl carrying a pitcher.

"Child, could you guide me to the house of Alcinoüs, lord among these people?" Odysseus asked, standing before her. "I come from a far land, a distant country, and I don't know anyone."

"Yes, sir, I will gladly show you the house, because Alcinoüs lives near my own father. But follow in silence. I will lead the way. Don't question anybody because the people here are not patient with strangers."

Athena led the way and he followed. The Phaeacians did not notice him because of the mist. Odysseus marvelled at the harbours and the ships and the meeting places, and at the high walls surrounding the city, crowned with palisades. They came to the palace of the king.

"Here, Sir, is the house that you asked about," said the disguised Athena. "You will find the king and his men feasting at a banquet. Go inside and

don't be afraid of anything. The first person you will come upon is the queen. Her name is Aretê. She is wise and settles quarrels between men. If you win her favour, there is hope you may return to your native land."

So saying, Athena departed and left the island. Odysseus stood before the palace of Alcinoüs. The high roof gleamed as bright as the sun or the moon, and the walls were made of bronze, surmounted by lapis lazuli. The outer doors were of gold and the doorposts were silver, set in a threshold of bronze. The lintel above was silver and the handle was gold. On either side of the door stood gold and silver dogs that Hephaestus himself, the god of crafts, had fashioned to guard the palace. They were ageless, immortal.

Inside, seats were fixed along the walls on either side from the threshold to the central hall, and on these seats were robes of fine fabric, the handiwork of Phaeacian women. The leaders of the Phaeacians liked to sit here drinking and eating, for they lived in unfailing abundance. Golden youths stood on pedestals holding lighted torches, giving light by night to banqueters in the hall. There were fifty slave women in the house, some grinding grain on millstones and others weaving fabrics, busy as rustling leaves on a tall birch. The Phaeacian women were cunning weavers at the loom, as skilled in their craft as the Phaeacian men were skilled above all others in speeding over the sea.

Outside, close to the doors, was a large courtyard. A hedge ran around it. Inside grew all kinds of trees: luxuriant pears and pomegranates, apples, figs and olives. These fruits never failed in winter or summer but lasted throughout the year, apple ripening on apple and grape on grape and fig on fig. There was a vineyard, one part on level ground spread with drying grapes, and another part filled with men gathering the grapes and treading on them. Next to the last row of vines were garden beds of every kind, blooming all year long, and in the orchard two springs, one sending water through the garden while the other flowed to the house. Such were the glorious gifts of the gods!

Odysseus stood and marvelled at the house. Then he passed quickly through the hall, still wrapped in the thick mist that Athena had shed on him. He came to Aretê and Alcinoüs, the king, and he threw his arms about the knees of Aretê. At that instant the mist disappeared.

A hush fell on the room at the sight of him and the Phaeacians wondered at the vision.

"Aretê, I've come to you and to your husband and to your knees as a suppliant," Odysseus said. "I have suffered greatly. May the gods grant you your every wish and grant that your men pass on their wealth and honours to their children. But give me speedy conveyance, I beg, to my native land, and quickly! I have long suffered troubles, far from my people."

He sat down in the ashes next to the fire. Finally, a Phaeacian leader spoke and said, addressing the room, "Alcinoüs, this is not the proper way, that a stranger should sit on the ground in the ashes! Come, raise the stranger to his feet and set him on a chair. Bid the slaves mix wine and let us all pour to Zeus who favours suppliants!"

Alcinoüs took Odysseus by the hand and raised him up from the hearth. He set him on a chair where his son Laodamus had sat, his most beloved child who always seated next to him. A servant brought in water in a pitcher of gold and poured it over a silver basin to wash Odysseus' hands. She drew up a table beside him. Another slave set out bread and all kinds of delicacies. Odysseus ate and drank.

"Pontonoüs, mix up some wine and serve it to everybody so that we may pour to Zeus, who supports all suppliants," declared Alcinoüs in a booming voice.

Pontonoüs mixed the wine and served it to everybody. When they had poured offerings and drunk to their hearts' content, Alcinoüs addressed the room:

"Listen to me, leaders of the Phaeacians. Finish your feasting, then go to your homes and sleep. In the morning we'll consider how we can carry this

stranger to his native land, even if it is far away. Of course, what happens then is up to the Fates, the dread spinners who spun out a thread for him at birth! Always show kindness to strangers, as they may be gods in disguise. Although the gods don't usually come to us in disguise, because we're close kin to them, like the Cyclopes and the wild Giants from whom we descend."

"Banish that thought from your minds," Odysseus answered. "I am not like the gods who live in the sky: I am a man. Think of the man you know who has suffered most of all men, and that is who I am like – and I could tell a long story. For now, let me eat, for hunger makes its own demands, and even if a man is sad with grief, as I am sad, yet his belly bids him forget. But at dawn send me forth, please."

The Phaeacians praised his words and urged that he be sent on his way. Then each man went to his house to take his rest. Odysseus was alone in the hall except for Aretê and Alcinoüs. The servants cleared the dishes. Aretê was first to speak, recognizing Odysseus' tunic and cloak as beautiful clothes she herself had made.

"Stranger, I want to ask you these questions first. Who are you and where do you come from? Who gave you these clothes? Didn't you say you came here wandering over the sea?"

"It would be hard, my queen, to tell you my sufferings, for the gods have given me many, but I'll tell you this. There's an island called Ogygia, far off in the sea. There dwells Calypso, the daughter of Atlas – deceitful Calypso, a dread goddess who lives apart from gods and mortals! Fate brought me to her house. Zeus hit my ship with a thunderbolt and shattered it in the middle of the sea. All my comrades died, but I grabbed the keel and drifted for nine days. On the tenth night, the gods brought me to Ogygia.

"Calypso took me into her house and gave me food and said she would make me immortal. But she could not persuade me. I remained there for seven years and always my tears wet the clothes that Calypso gave me. But when the eighth year came, she urged me to go, either because she got a message from Zeus or because she changed her mind. Whatever the reason, she sent me to sea on a raft and she gave me provisions, bread, wine and clothing, and she made a gentle wind blow. For seventeen days I sailed. On the eighteenth, the shadowy mountains of your land appeared before me. My heart was glad, but Poseidon was not yet done with me. Poseidon stirred up the winds and monstrously roused the sea. My raft groaned and was shattered by the storm, but I managed to swim my way through the sea until the wind and waves brought me here.

"I wanted to scramble onto land, but the waves would have dashed me against the rocks on the shore. Instead, I swam until I came to a river with smooth rocks and shelter. I sank down, gasping for breath, and night came on. I lay down to rest, gathering leaves about me, and I fell into a deep sleep the whole night through until morning and then midday, when the sun turned to go down. It was then I heard a shout and awoke. I saw the handmaids of your daughter playing ball on the shore, and in the middle was your daughter, looking like Artemis. She gave me bread and wine, and bathed me in the river and gave me these clothes too."

"Stranger, I don't think that my daughter acted rightly in this," Alcinoüs answered. "She should have brought you to our house right away!"

"Sir, please don't rebuke your daughter. I see no fault in her. She asked me to follow along with her handmaids, but I didn't think it would be a good idea, fearing that you could be angry. Humans are quick to anger, I think."

"Stranger, it's not my way to get angry over nothing," Alcinoüs said. "Measure in all matters is preferable. I would rather that you, being the kind of man you are, and of like mind with me . . . that you might marry my daughter and be called my son and remain here! I'd give you a house and possessions, if you chose to remain. But no Phaeacian will keep you away from your goal."

Odysseus was happy and spoke to himself in prayer: "Zeus, grant that Alcinoüs bring to pass what he has said. His fame will never die over the entire earth, and I shall get home!"

Aretê told her slaves to set up a bed underneath the portico and to heap blankets on it and covers and quilts. The handmaids went out carrying torches. When they had made up the bed, they came to Odysseus and said, "Come now, stranger, go to your rest. Your bed is ready."

He was happy to lie down on the corded bedstead beneath the echoing portico. King Alcinoüs, meanwhile, lay down in the innermost chamber of his house, and beside him lay his wife Aretê.

Book 8

THE LOVE AFFAIR BETWEEN ARES AND APHRODITE

Dawn broke over the city. Alcinoüs led the way to the place of assembly, while Athena walked through the streets disguised as Alcinoüs' messenger. She went up to each man she passed and said:

"Come now, Sir, make your way to the place of assembly, so that you may learn about the stranger who has arrived at the palace."

She aroused their curiosity, and the assembly place was soon filled. They marvelled at the sight of Odysseus, for Athena had shed grace on his head and shoulders.

Alcinoüs addressed the assembled crowd. "Listen to me, leaders of the Phaeacians. This stranger – whoever he might be – prays for our help. Let us draw a ship down to the sea and choose fifty-two of our best sailors. I will prepare a feast for you all. And summon Demodocus, who delights listeners with his songs."

Fifty-two sailors were selected and they went down to the shore. They drew the ship into deep water, fitted the mast and sail, and fastened the oars to the thole straps. Then they lowered the ship into the channel.

The sailors made their way back to the palace. The porticos, courts and rooms were filled with men, young and old. Alcinoüs slaughtered twelve sheep, eight boars and two oxen, and a great feast was prepared.

The messenger boy arrived with the singer, Demodocus. The Muse loved this man above all others and bestowed him with both good and terrible fortune. She deprived him of his sight, but gave him the gift of song through his beautiful voice.

Everybody set to the feast with good cheer. When they had finished, the Muse moved the minstrel to sing of the famous quarrel between Odysseus and Achilles, the time when they argued violently at a feast.

As he listened to the song, Odysseus took his purple cloak in his powerful hands and drew it over his head to hide his face, for he was ashamed of his tears. Alcinoüs, sitting next to him, realized he was crying.

"Hear me, leaders of the Phaeacians!" Alcinoüs said. "We have eaten our fill. Now let us try our strength, so this stranger may tell his friends how we excel in boxing, wrestling, jumping and running."

Alcinoüs led the way to the place of assembly and a great throng followed, including Alcinoüs' three sons: Laodamas, Halius and Clytoneüs. Euryalus also joined them, a Phaeacian second only to Laodamas in strength and good looks.

First of all, a race was laid out and they all raised the dust as they sprinted, but Clytoneüs was by far the best, and he shot to the front. Next, they tried wrestling, at which Euryalus excelled. Another Phaeacian won the high jump, and someone else threw the discus the farthest. In the boxing, Laodamas came out on top.

"Come, my friends, let us ask this stranger whether he's an athlete," said Alcinoüs' son Laodamas. "He's no weed – muscular thighs and calves, and a strong neck and arms, too."

Laodamas went up to Odysseus. "Come join us," he urged. "Cast away all care! It won't delay your journey long. Your ship is launched and the crew is ready."

"Laodamas," replied Odysseus, "my mind is filled with sorrow, longing for home and praying to your king and your people."

Euryalus taunted him. "Well, stranger, you certainly don't look as

though you could hold your own in games. You look more like a merchant who thinks only of his cargo and how much he can greedily siphon off."

"Sir, your words are ill-judged," Odysseus answered with an angry glance. "Your rude speech has riled me. When I was young, I was the best, but now I'm ruined by the suffering I've endured in warfare and on the dangerous waves. Nonetheless, I'll give you a go, for your words sting me."

Odysseus leaped up. He took hold of the thickest, heaviest discus, far larger than those the Phaeacians had used. Spinning around, he let go, and the discus hummed as it flew. The Phaeacians fell to the ground, frightened by the rushing of the stone.

"Try this now, my friends!" he said with a lightened heart. "I'll send another as far, or farther. As for the other games, if you want to put me to the test, let's do it – boxing, wrestling, sprinting. The only thing I won't do is compete with Laodamas, son of Alcinoüs. A man who challenges his host is a fool. But I refuse no other Phaeacian. I know how to shoot a bow. When we were in Troy, only Philoctetes was a superior shot. I can throw a spear farther than most men can shoot an arrow. It's only in the running race that I fear some of you may beat me, for I have lost fitness on my travels over the seas."

The Phaeacians were hushed into silence.

"Stranger, well said," responded Alcinoüs. "The way this man so openly taunted you was highly uncivilized! But I hope that when you're back feasting in your halls you will tell tales of *our* skills, which we enjoy thanks to Zeus. We're fast sprinters and we are the best seamen. We like to banquet and we enjoy good song; we love to dance and wear fine clothes and take warm baths and go to bed.

"So come forwards, the best dancers among the Phaeacians, so that the stranger may tell his friends when he gets home how we excel in dance and seamanship as well as in sprinting and song. Somebody find Demodocus again! His lyre is in our halls."

A slave rose to fetch the lyre from the palace while nine carefully chosen men took charge of the dance. When the slave returned with the lyre, Demodocus took it and stepped into the middle of the circle, and young boys took up their positions around him. Demodocus struck the strings and the boys beat the dance floor with agile feet.

When the dancing was over, the minstrel sang of the love affair of Ares and Aphrodite. Ares had heaped gifts on Aphrodite and he shamed Hephaestus' marriage bed. But Helios, the sun god, let Hephaestus know about the affair. Hephaestus went into his workshop, consumed with evil thoughts. On the anvil he forged a chain that could not be broken. Then he went into his bedroom and spread the chain round about the bedpost, making a web as fine as a spider's. Not even a god could have seen it, it was so cunningly fashioned. When he had spread his snare around the bed, he made it known he was going to the island of Lemnos. When Ares heard this, he went to Hephaestus' house, eager to make love to Aphrodite.

"Come, my love, let us go to bed and have a little fun!" he said, clasping her hand. "Hephaestus is not here. He has gone to Lemnos."

She liked his suggestion very much, so they went up to bed and lay down together. The cunning chains of Hephaestus fell on them so they could not sit up or even move. They realized they could never escape.

Hephaestus, whose legs were lame, stood now in the doorway. Fierce anger seized him. He cried out terribly to the gods:

"Father Zeus, and all you other gods, come and get a good look! Aphrodite, Zeus' daughter, shames me because I am lame. She loves that handsome Ares because he is strong of limb – but I came into the world misshapen. You will see how they've gone up to my bed. They sleep together while I stand by full to the brim with grief. You know, I don't think they'll want to stay much longer like this, no matter how attracted to each other they are. The chains shall hold them fast until her father pays back the gifts that I gave for his cruel daughter!"

The gods came to his house: Poseidon, Hermes and Apollo, the farshooter. They stood in the doorway and roared with laughter together. One god glanced at another and said:

"Ha! Evil deeds never win! The tortoise overtakes the hare, just as Hephaestus has caught Ares! Ares will now pay for his adultery!"

But Apollo turned to Hermes. "Hermes, Zeus' son, guide of the gods, giver of good things, would you be happy to lie in bed beside Aphrodite even if it meant being trapped in chains?"

"I wish I suffered this," Hermes answered. "I wish that three times as many bonds might hold me, and all the gods and goddesses look on, if only I could sleep by the side of Aphrodite."

The immortal gods laughed, apart from Poseidon who kept asking Hephaestus to set Ares free. "Let him go and I promise that he will pay you all that he owes," Poseidon insisted.

"Don't ask this, Poseidon," Hephaestus answered. "It is a sorry thing to be surety for a rat. How could I put you, one of the gods, in bonds if Ares should avoid the payment?"

"Hephaestus, if Ares refuses to pay, then I will pay you myself," said Poseidon.

"Well, I cannot refuse you; nor would it be right."

Hephaestus loosened the bonds. Freed, the two lovers sprang up instantly and fled in shame.

This was the song the minstrel sang, and Odysseus enjoyed listening very much, as did the Phaeacians.

Then Alcinoüs asked Halius and Laodamas to dance, because they were the best. They took a beautiful ball of purple yarn and one tossed it to the clouds while the other leaped up and caught it before touching the ground. On they danced, tossing the ball back and forth, while other Phaeacian youths stood in the background and beat time. The applause was thunderous.

"Lord Alcinoüs, famous above all men, you told us that your dancers were the best," Odysseus said, "and now I believe you."

Instantly Alcinoüs stood up and addressed the Phaeacians.

"Hear me, leaders and councillors of the Phaeacians, I believe this man is no fool! Let us give him a gift of friendship, as is fitting. I want each of you to bring a freshly washed cloak, a tunic and a bar of gold. Let us offer them all together so that the stranger may go with a glad heart. And I would like Euryalus to apologize to the stranger and give him a gift also. For he did not address him appropriately.

Each of the lords sent a man to his house to retrieve the gifts.

"Lord, I will make amends as you ask," Euryalus said. "And I will give him this sword. It's entirely bronze and the hilt is silver. It has a scabbard of freshly sawn ivory, an object of great worth." He placed the silver-studded sword into Odysseus' hands. "Stranger, if I have said anything harsh," Euryalus said, "may the storm winds blow it away. And may the gods help you to see your wife again and your native land. You've been on the road a long time."

"Well, hail to you, my friend," Odysseus said, "and may the gods give you happiness . . . and may you never want for this sword that you've given me in your apology."

"Wife, bring a chest out here, the best you have," Alcinoüs said, "and place inside it a cloak and tunic for the stranger. Now put a cauldron on the fire to warm some water for his bath. When he is bathed and has seen the gifts, he can enjoy the feast and hear a good song. And I will give him this cup of mine, made of gold, so he may remember me as he pours offerings to Zeus and the other gods."

Aretê asked her house-slaves to set up a cauldron. They filled it with water and kindled wood beneath it. The fire played around the belly of the vessel and the water grew warm.

In the meantime, Aretê brought out a beautiful chest from the treasure room. She placed the clothes and the gold inside it.

"Now put on the lid and tie it with a cord," she said to Odysseus. "Otherwise someone may rob you when you are lying asleep as you travel."

Odysseus secured the lid right away and tied a cord around the chest, employing a cunning knot he had learned from Circe. When the slaves had bathed him and rubbed his flesh with oil and had put on him a tunic and cloak, he went to join the men drinking wine in the hall. The beautiful Nausicaa stood near the doorpost. She was astonished when she saw Odysseus.

"Farewell, stranger, and remember me in your native land."

"Nausicaa, daughter of Alcinoüs, may Zeus grant that I come to my home. Then I will pray to you as to a goddess, for you have given me life."

Odysseus went inside and sat down next to Alcinoüs. A slave entered, leading in Demodocus, honoured by all. And so everybody set happily to the feast.

"Demodocus," said Odysseus when they had eaten their fill, "I don't know whether you learned from the Muse or from Apollo, but you seem to know what happened to the Achaeans. Sing of the wooden horse that Odysseus led into Troy, filled with the men who would burn down the city. If you can tell me this story, I will declare to all that a god has given you this power of divine song."

Demodocus, moved by the Muse, began. He took up the tale at the point where the Achaeans were sailing away after burning their huts while a few others, led by Odysseus, were in the plaza of Troy, hidden in the wooden horse. The Trojans couldn't decide what to do with it. There were three suggestions: to chop it up, or drag it to the heights and throw it onto the rocks, or just to let it stand, as an offering to the immortal gods. For it was the Trojans' fate to perish once the city enclosed the wooden horse. There crouched the best of the Achaeans, about to bring death to all.

And the minstrel sang about how the Achaeans came out of the horse and sacked the city. He told how Odysseus went to the house of Deïphobus, who married Helen when Paris died. Odysseus went in the company of Menelaüs. The fight was savage but Odysseus was victorious.

Odysseus' heart melted when he heard this and tears fell on his cheeks. He wept as profoundly as a woman who wails and throws herself on her dead husband, fallen before his city in his attempt to stave off doom; she clings and shrieks as she looks on him dying and gasping for breath, even as the enemy beats her back with their spears and leads her away, her cheeks wrecked with sorrow. This is how the tears fell onto Odysseus' cheeks. He concealed them from those around him, but Alcinoüs saw them.

"Hear me, leaders of the Phaeacians," Alcinoüs announced. "Demodocus, stop playing now. Everything we have done here, arranging transportation and giving gifts, has been in the stranger's honour. For a stranger and a suppliant is as dear as a brother to anyone with any sense.

"I'm going to ask you questions, stranger, and I don't want you to cleverly conceal the truth. It's better to speak out. Tell me your name. What do they call you at home, your mother and father and townsmen? For everybody has a name! And tell me your country and your people and your city so our ships may send you there. The Phaeacians have no need for pilots or ships with steering oars like other nations, for our ships know the thoughts of men, and they know the cities and fields of all peoples and the vastness of the seas that they cross, hidden in mist. They never fear shipwreck.

"Yet I once heard this story from my father. He used to say that Poseidon was angry because we give transportation to all men. He said that someday a Phaeacian ship would return from a trip over the sea and Poseidon would strike her, then hide our city behind a mountain. So the old man said. Of course, it's up to the gods whether these things come to pass, or whether we escape this fate.

"But come, tell me truly, where you have wandered and what countries you have seen. Tell me of the people and their towns, of those who were cruel and wild and unjust, and of those who were kind to strangers. And tell me why you weep when you hear of the doom of the Achaeans and of Troy. Did some kinsmen of yours fall in front of Troy? Maybe your daughter's husband or your wife's father? Or was it perhaps a friend dear to you?"

Book 9

THE CAVE OF THE CYCLOPS

So spoke Odysseus:

Lord Alcinoüs, famous above all men, you want to know my story. Where shall I begin? Misfortunes too numerous to count have befallen me. First, let me tell you my name. I hope that someday I may entertain you in my own home, though it is far away. I am Odysseus, the son of Laertes.

I live in Ithaca. There is a mountain there called Neriton, covered with forest that you can see from far distant. It's a rugged island but a good place to raise young men. Calypso kept me in her caves, and the witch Circe detained me on her island, too. But they could not persuade me to want to stay with them. The truth is there is nothing sweeter than a man's own land, and his own parents, not even a luxurious home when it's far away in a foreign land.

Let me recount the misfortunes that Zeus has laid upon me.

From Troy the wind carried us to Thrace and to Ismarus, town of the Cicones. We sacked the city and put the men to death. We took the wives and piles of gold and divided the takings among us. I said we should get out of there fast, but others would not listen. We drank a lot of wine and feasted plentifully on sheep and cattle.

Meanwhile, the Cicones summoned nearby tribes, who lived inland – good fighters, both with chariots and on foot. Huge numbers of them suddenly appeared, like the leaves and flowers that bloom in the spring at dawn. An evil fate befell us. We set up a battle line by the ships and hurled our spears. We held our ground all through the morning, but in the

afternoon the Cicones prevailed and routed us. Six men died from every ship, which only carried twenty to begin with. The rest of us escaped.

For nine days, the savage winds carried me, but on the tenth, we came to the land of the Lotus Eaters. We went ashore and drew water and fixed a meal by the ships. When we had satisfied our hunger, I sent out some men to scout. I nominated two, and a third as a messenger. They went off and mingled with the Lotus Eaters, who gave them honey-sweet fruit to enjoy. And when they tasted the lotus, they no longer wanted to come back. They wished to remain with the Lotus Eaters, all thoughts of home forgotten. I dragged these men back to the ships myself, tying them beneath the benches. I ordered the rest of my men to leave as quickly as possible. We sat down on the ship's benches and struck the sea with our oars.

We came to the land of the Cyclopes, a savage and lawless people. They live on the tops of mountains in big caves. Each one is commander of his children and his wives. There's another island beyond the harbour of the Cyclopes' island, a fertile one. Countless wild goats live there. There are no men on the island to hunt them; nobody tramps the mountain peaks in

their pursuit. There are no flocks of sheep, no ploughed lands. The island is empty of humankind. There are just plenty of goats . . .

The island has a harbour so calm you don't need to anchor your ship; you can simply draw it up on shore. And the breezes blow fair. At the head of the harbour is a spring flowing from beneath a cave surrounded by birches. We sailed in there. We went at night when a mist lay over the ships and the moon was hidden by cloud. We couldn't see the waves on the beach until we had run our ships up on shore. We lowered the sails and waited for dawn.

When dawn broke, we roamed through the island and were amazed. Some nymphs, the daughters of Zeus, stirred up the meat of the mountain goats so that my men might have a meal. We took our curved bows and spears from the ships and at once found plenty of game.

All day long we feasted and drank sweet wine. We looked across the water to the land of the Cyclopes and saw smoke rising. We heard the sounds of sheep and goats. When the sun set, we lay down on the shore. When dawn appeared I called my men together and said, "I'll go with my own ship and crew to test out these men across the way, to learn whether they are cruel, savage and unjust or whether they are kind to strangers, and if they fear the gods."

I got on board and my men struck the sea with their oars. When we reached the Cyclopes' land we spotted a high cave near the edge of the water, roofed with laurel branches. There were crowds of sheep and goats penned in there for the night. In front of the cave there was a stone courtyard. Tall pines and oaks grew all around. For sure, a huge man slept here at night, a marvellous monstrosity, not like a man that lives by bread, but more like the peak of lofty mountains, covered in woods, which stands out apart from the rest.

I told most of my men to stay by the ship, but I chose twelve of my best to accompany me. I carried with me a skin of dark sweet wine that I had received from Maro, a priest of Apollo at Ismarus, because we protected him and his child and wife during the sack of Ismarus. You could take one cup and pour it into twenty of water and a heavenly smell would rise from the mixing bowl.

We came to the cave, but the shepherd was with his flocks in the fields. We went inside and looked with wonder at crates filled with cheeses and pens crowded with lambs and kids. Surrounding the pens were all the many vessels into which he milked the animals.

My men begged me to take some of the cheese and the goats and lambs and sail away. But I did not listen. I hoped that I could see the man himself and that he might welcome me with gifts.

We started a fire and offered sacrifice and we took some of the cheeses and ate them. We sat in the cave and waited until the owner, a giant with one eye, came back from herding his flocks. He carried a huge weight of dry wood and threw it down with a crash. We were terrified and huddled back into a recess. He drove his fat flocks into the cave. Then he placed in the doorway a stone so huge that twenty-two wagons could not lift it. He sat down and milked the lambs and goats in turn. He separated half the white milk into curds and gathered them in wicker baskets; the other half of the milk he placed in vessels so he could drink it for dinner. When he finished, he started up the fire and he saw us.

"Strangers, who are you?" he asked. "Where do you come from, sailing over the sea? Are you on some business or do you wander around like pirates risking their own lives and terrorizing different lands?"

So he spoke, and our spirit was broken at his voice. Even so, I answered:

"We, if you'd like to know, are from Troy. We've been driven by the winds, trying to get home. We are Agamemnon's men, whose fame is greatest under heaven because he's sacked a great city. But we come as suppliants and hope you will be generous, as is right in the treatment of strangers."

At once, pitilessly, he answered: "You are a fool, stranger, or you come from a long way off, seeing that you ask me to fear the gods! The Cyclopes pay no attention to Zeus or other gods because we are better than they. But tell me, where did you land your ship? Was it in a remote part of the island or nearby?"

He was testing me, but I wasn't tricked!

"Poseidon smashed my ship to pieces," I answered craftily. "He threw her on the rocks at the edge of your land. But I escaped with these men."

He made no answer. He seized two of my men and dashed them to the earth as if they were puppies, and their brains flowed onto the ground. Then he cut them up limb from limb and ate them as if he were a mountain lion, leaving nothing at all, the guts, the flesh, the bones, the marrow. Wailing, we held up our hands to Zeus when we saw this cruelty! We were helpless.

But when the Cyclops – whose name was Polyphemus, I later learned – had filled his belly with human flesh, washing it down with milk, he lay down in the cave, stretched out among the sheep. I planned to sneak up near him, draw my sharp sword and stab him in the breast. Then I realized that we would die in the cave, because we could not throw back the rock from the door! So, lamenting, we waited for daybreak.

At dawn the Cyclops started up the fire again and milked his animals. When he finished, he seized two of my men and prepared his meal. When he was done eating, he drove his flocks out of the cave. He had no problem moving the big rock, then putting it back, the way you might set the lid on a quiver. I was left there, devising some way I could take revenge.

Next to the sheep pen lay a great club of olive wood, as large as the mast of a ship, that the Cyclops had cut to carry with him. I hacked off about a six-foot length and sharpened the point. Then I hardened it in the blazing fire and concealed it in dung. I told my men to cast lots to see who would come with me to grind the stake into the Cyclops' eye once he fell asleep. The lot fell on four good men, and I was the fifth.

When evening came, the Cyclops herded his animals into the cave. He lifted up the rock and placed it in the doorway, then, sitting down, milked the ewes and goats. When he was done, he again seized two of my men. He smashed their heads, cut them up and ate them. I came up close to the Cyclops, holding a wooden bowl of the sweet dark wine from Ismarus.

"Cyclops, here, have some wine, now that you've had your meal, so you may know what kind of drink we had on our ship. I was bringing it to you as an offering because I hoped you would take pity on me and send me home. But you are raging in a way that is unbearable!"

He took the cup of wine and drained it, very pleased with the sweet liquor. "Give it to me again," he said, "and tell me your name so that I may give you a welcome gift. For this is a divine drink."

I handed him the wine again. Three times I gave it and three times he drank it down. When the wine had clouded his wits, I spoke to him:

"Cyclops, you've asked my name and I will tell it to you, and you can give me a welcome gift as you promised. My name is Nobdy."

At once he answered: "Nobdy, I'll eat you last. This shall be your welcome gift."

Reclining, he fell on his back and lay there with his neck bent in a slant.

Sleep, the conqueror, took hold. He vomited wine and human flesh in his drunken slumber. I got out the stake from the dung and put the end in the fire. I bolstered up my men so nobody would be afraid. When the olive wood glowed terribly, I pulled it from the heat. My men stood around me and a god breathed courage in us.

I took the stake and buried it in the Cyclops' eye, throwing all my weight on it from above. I whirled it around like a man bores timber with a drill, and the drill runs on and on. We twisted the fiery pointed stake in his eye, and the blood burbled around it. An axe or an adze makes a great hissing sound when the smith dips it in cold water to temper it; this is how the Cyclops' eye sizzled around the stake. He screamed and the rock rang with the sound.

Terrified, we shrank back as he wrenched the stake from his eye, fouled with blood. He flung it off himself and shouted to the Cyclopes who lived in caves nearby. Hearing his cry, they came thronging from every side and asked:

"What is the problem, Polyphemus, that you cry out through the night, keeping us awake?"

"My friends, Nobdy is killing me."

"Well, if no one is harming you, you must have a sickness, and that's thanks to Zeus. You must pray to our father, Lord Poseidon."

The other Cyclopes went off. My heart laughed inside me. Groaning in anguish, the Cyclops groped with his hands and removed the stone from the door and sat in the doorway with his arms outstretched, hoping to catch anyone who tried to get out.

I needed to devise a way of escape. I thought of all kinds of things. This seemed the best plan. There were plenty of rams, wonderful animals, and large. I bound them together in threes, and beneath each middle animal, I secured one of my men. As for me, there was a boss ram, far the best of the flock. I took hold of the wool on his back and curled under his belly. I lay there with my face up, clinging to his fleece.

When dawn came, the males of the flock pushed out to pasture and the females bleated, unmilked in their pens. The Cyclops, in agony, felt the backs of the sheep as they came past, but he did not see that my men were bound beneath. Last of all the ram went out with me hanging on.

"My precious ram, why are you the last to go out?" he asked. "The sheep have never left you behind before, you are always first. But now you're at the very back. You must be sorry for your master, blinded by an evil man, that person named Nobdy, who I tell you has not yet escaped. If only you could feel as I do and learn to speak and tell me where he is hiding . . . then I'd dash his brains all over the cave, and my heart would be lightened."

So saying, he sent the ram out the door. When we had gone a little way from the cave I let go and quickly untied my men. We drove forwards the sheep, rich in fat. Our comrades were glad to see we had escaped, but they wept for the six men the Cyclops had eaten. The men sat down on the ship's benches and struck the sea with their oars.

When I was as far away as a man's voice carries, I shouted to the Cyclops, who stood near his cave:

"Cyclops! Your evil deeds fell on your own head, you who did not hesitate to eat your own guests in your own house. Zeus has taken revenge on you."

He became still more angry and broke off the top of a high mountain and threw it. It fell in front of the ship. The sea swelled beneath the stone and carried the ship back towards the land. But I took a long pole and shoved it off, and I told my men to get to their oars and get us out of there.

When we were twice as distant as before, I began again to call to the Cyclops, though my men tried to stop me, saying, "Stubborn man! Why do you provoke this savage who just now has hurled a stone into the sea that drove our ship back to the land?"

But they could not dissuade me. Full of anger, I shouted again:

"Cyclops, if any man asks you about your eye, say that Odysseus, the sacker of cities, blinded it: Odysseus, the son of Laertes."

Then he prayed to Poseidon, stretching out his hands to the sky. "Hear me, Poseidon, shaker of the earth, god with the dark hair, if I am really your son and you are really my father, grant that Odysseus may never reach his home! But if it's fated that he should see his native land, may he reach it late and in agony after losing all his men. And may he find trouble in his house!"

The Cyclops lifted a far larger stone and swung it and threw it with tremendous strength. It landed just behind the ship, and the wave bore us to the other island where the rest of our fleet was beached. We pulled our ship up on the sands. We drove out the herds we'd taken from the Cyclops and divided them so that no man would go without. My men gave me the big ram. On the shore I cut his throat in honour of Zeus, and I burned the thigh pieces.

All day long we feasted on the wine and flesh, and when the sun set we lay down on the shore. As soon as dawn rose, I roused my men.

From there we sailed on, grieving for our loss of six men, but glad we had escaped death.

Book 10

CIRCE

Odysseus continued his tale:

We came to the island of Aeolus, a man much loved by the gods. We were entertained for an entire month. Aeolus questioned me about everything, especially Troy. I told him all that I knew. And when finally I asked him if I could leave, he gave me a bag made from the hide of a nine-year-old ox, in which he bound the raging winds. Zeus had made him keeper of the winds, able to rouse them and quiet them at will. Aeolus tied the bag so tightly that not a trace of air could escape. Then he summoned for me West Wind to propel our ships and men on their way.

We sailed for nine days and nine nights, and on the tenth, Ithaca came in sight. We were so near that we saw men tending their fires along the shore. I fell asleep, tired because I had been handling the sail myself for the entire journey. But my men began to complain, saying that the big black bag was filled with gold and silver that I planned to take home.

"Wherever he goes, Odysseus finds fortune!" they said. "He has so much beautiful treasure from Troy, and now Aeolus has given him even more! Let's see how much gold and silver there is in the bag."

So they opened it up, and out rushed the winds. In an instant, a storm seized our boats and carried us out to sea, far from my native land. The wicked blast drove us back to Aeolus' island. They were amazed to see us and asked, "What are you doing here, Odysseus? What cruel god has attacked you? We sent you off with every care, so that you might get home in one piece."

I said, "My wicked men have ruined me. But heal us, my friends, for you have the power!"

They were silent. Then Aeolus answered, "Cursed man, get off this island right away! Go, for you come here as one hated by the gods!"

For six days and nights we sailed on, and on the seventh we came to the stronghold of the Laestrygonians. We arrived at a fine harbour. On both sides, steep cliffs rose sheer at the mouth's narrow entrance. Eleven of my ships steered into the harbour and moored there. I alone moored outside the harbour, fastening my cables to a rock.

I despatched three men to find out who lived in this place. At the edge of the city they met a girl drawing water, daughter of the Laestrygonian Antiphates. She took them right away to her father's house.

They went into the palace. Antiphates instantly seized one of my men and dashed out his brains, preparing to make a meal of him. The other two men raced back to the ship. Then the Laestrygonians started to appear from every side, a huge crowd, more like Giants than men!

They showered my fleet in the harbour with enormous rocks, and the terrible sounds of men dying and ships smashing rent the air. They speared some men as if they were fish, then took them home for a disgusting meal. While the Laestrygonians were killing those inside the harbour, I drew my sword and slashed the cables holding my ship, calling my men to man the oars. They churned up the sea with their blades, in fear of their lives, and we sped away. But the other ships and all their men were lost.

From there we sailed on. We came to the island of Aeaea where Circe lives, the daughter of Helios, the sun god. We put to shore in silence, our hearts weary with sorrow. I took my spear and sword and walked uphill from the ship to a place where I could get a clear view, hoping to see signs of men and hear their voices. Through the woods I spied smoke rising from the halls of Circe. I turned to go back so I could send my men there to find out what was going on.

"Now listen up, my men, in spite of your suffering. I climbed up high to an outlook. The sea surrounds the island like a wreath, but I did see smoke rising through the brush."

Their spirit was shattered when they heard me, remembering what the Laestrygonians had already done to our comrades, as well as the carnage of the man-eating Cyclops. They wailed and poured out tears.

I divided the men into two bands. I took command myself of one group, and the other I entrusted to Eurylochus, a relative. We shook lots in a bronze helmet and Eurylochus' lot leapt out. He set off with twenty-two men and left my group behind. They came to a meadow in the forest where they found a house made of polished stone, belonging to Circe. All around it wandered tame wolves and lions that she had bewitched. Instead of rushing my men, these animals wagged their tails and stood on their hind legs, the way a dog greets his master when he comes home from a party carrying morsels of meat. All the same, my men were terrified, and they crowded into the courtyard in front of the goddess' house.

From inside the house they heard Circe singing. "Men, someone is singing as she weaves," said Polites, a natural leader, "and the halls echo. Let's call her."

Circe opened the shining doors and invited them to enter. They followed her in. Only Eurylochus, suspecting a trap, stayed behind. She had them sit on chairs. Then she gave them all drinks – but she mixed them with evil drugs.

When she served them the potion, they swallowed it straight away. Then she struck them with her wand and penned them in pigsties. They had the heads, voices and bristles of pigs, but their minds were unaltered. So they were penned there, weeping, and Circe cast acorns and nuts before them, and the fruit of the dogwood – feed enjoyed by wallowing swine.

But Eurylochus came back to the ship. He could hardly talk; he wanted only to weep. He managed to tell us the fate of his comrades – that they had vanished inside a beautiful palace. "Not one came out again," he said, "though I sat for a long time and watched."

When I heard his words, I put my sword around my shoulders, a sword made of bronze, and I slung my bow about me. I asked Eurylochus to lead me to the palace, but he grasped my knees and, wailing, begged:

"Don't take me there against my will! I know that you will never return, and nor will you bring back your men. No, let's get out of here with those who remain . . . We may still escape this evil!"

"Eurylochus, stay here. But I will go. I must."

I made my way inland, and as I was walking through the forest, Hermes met me, in the likeness of a young man with his first down on his lip.

"Why, sad man, do you walk alone through these hills?" he asked, taking hold of my hand. "Your comrades are transformed into pigs. Are you going to set them free? Come, I will keep you safe from harm. Here, take this herb and it will ward off evil. Circe will mix a potion and put drugs into it. However, she will not be able to charm you because of this herb that I give you. When Circe strikes you with her wand, instantly draw your sword and rush upon her as though you are going to kill her. She will be frightened and will ask you to go to bed with her. Don't refuse: go along with it in order to free your men, and be taken care of yourself. Ask her to swear an oath that she will not plot against you, for otherwise when she has you naked she will cut off your genitals."

Hermes gave me a herb that he pulled from the ground. At its root it was black but the flower was milky. The gods call it *Moly*. Men can't dig it up but the gods can do anything. Hermes then left, and I went on my way to Circe's house. My thoughts were dark. I stood in the courtyard and called out and she heard my voice. She opened the doors and invited me in. I went inside, though I was uneasy.

Circe made me sit on a silver-studded chair, with a footstool beneath it. She prepared a potion and gave it to me to drink. When I had swallowed it, yet was not bewitched, she struck me with her wand.

"Go out to the sties and lie with the rest of your men!" she said.

I drew my sword and rushed upon her as if I meant to kill her. She cried aloud and seized my knees, beseeching me:

"Who are you and where do you come from?" she said. "No other man has withstood this charm. You can only be Odysseus, the man of many tricks, who Hermes once said would come here on his way back from Troy. So now, put your sword away and let us go to bed. By making love we may come to trust one another."

"How can you ask me to be gentle with you?" I replied. "You've turned my men into pigs and now, with treacherous intent, you invite me into your chamber? Once you strip me naked you may cut off my genitals. I don't want to get into your bed, goddess, unless you swear a mighty oath that you will not plot to do me harm."

She did swear the oath. Then we went to bed.

Her handmaids, meanwhile, were busy in the hall. There were four of them, the offspring of the springs and woods and rivers. One threw beautiful rugs on chairs and another brought tables of silver and set golden baskets on them, and the third mixed wine in a silver bowl and set out cups. The fourth brought water.

In the bathing area they kindled a big fire beneath a cauldron. When the water warmed, Circe bathed me, mixing the water to just the right temperature and pouring it over my head and shoulders. Then she put about me a tunic and cloak and brought me back into the hall where she made me sit down. A handmaid brought water in a pitcher to wash my hands, pouring it over a basin. She drew up a table. The housekeeper brought out bread and meats. Circe asked me to eat but I did not want to. Rather I sat thinking of other things, full of apprehension.

When Circe saw that I was not eating, because I was so burdened with grief, she said:

"Odysseus, why do you sit like this without touching your food? Do you think I may be up to some trick? Don't be afraid! I've sworn a mighty oath not to do you harm."

"Circe, what man could bring himself to eat food and drink before he'd set his men free? If you really mean it when you ask me to dine, release my men!"

Circe went out of the hall, holding her wand. She opened the doors of the pigsty and drove out the men in the form of swine. They stood before her and she walked among them, rubbing each one with a drug. Their bristles fell away and they became men again, younger than before, and better looking, and taller. They clung to my hands and descended into passionate sobs. The house rang with the sound of their weeping. The goddess herself was moved to pity.

"Odysseus, go now to your ship and draw it up on the land," she said. "Store your goods in a cave. Then come back and bring the rest of your men with you."

I went down to the ship and found my men wailing. When they saw me, they thronged around me, crying aloud, the way calves in a farmyard sport around the cows who come back to the yard, running around their mothers and lowing constantly.

"You have returned, Odysseus, and we are as glad as if we had reached Ithaca, our native land," they kept saying. "But what has happened to the other men?"

"First, let us get the ship up onto land and store our goods in a cave. Then follow me so you may see the others who are in the halls of Circe, drinking and eating."

They obeyed my words. Eurylochus alone held back.

"Ah, you dogs, where are you going?" he asked. "What, do you love these afflictions so much that you want to go to Circe's house and be changed into pigs or wolves or lions to guard her house? Remember how the Cyclops destroyed our men when we went into his cave? And who led them? Odysseus! It was because of his insanity that they died!"

I wondered whether I should draw my sword and cut off his head, though he was related to me by marriage. But my comrades stopped me.

"Odysseus, let us leave him alone. Let Eurylochus stay here and guard the ship while you lead us to Circe's house."

So saying, my men came with me, and Eurylochus came too, afraid of my rebuke.

Meanwhile, Circe had bathed the rest of my men and anointed them with oil and given them clothes. We found them dining together. When they saw us, they burst into tears and the house rang from their cries. Then beautiful Circe came near me.

"Son of Laertes, Odysseus of many wiles, let your torment go," Circe said. "I know all that you suffered on the sea and all the wrong that evil men have done you on land. But come now, eat the food and drink the wine so that you feel as vigorous as you did when you left your native land of Ithaca."

So she spoke, and in our proud hearts we agreed with her words. Day after day for a whole year we feasted. But when the year had passed, and the season turned so that the long days came again, my men called me out.

"It's time to remember your homeland at last!" they said. "It is destined that you reach your house and your native land!"

I agreed. All day long we feasted, but when the sun had set and it was time to lay down to sleep I went up to Circe and clutched her knees.

"Circe, I want you to deliver on the promise that you gave me, to send me home. I want to be gone now and so do my men, who wear me out as they sit around mourning whenever you are not here."

"Son of Laertes, Odysseus, first you must complete another journey. You must go to the House of Hades to seek a prophecy from the ghost of Teiresias of Thebes, the blind oracle."

My spirit was broken. I cried out and sank on the bed, no longer wishing to live. When I finished weeping, I answered:

"But Circe, who will be our guide? No man ever went to Hades' House in a black ship!"

"Don't worry about a pilot," she said. "Just set up your mast, spread your sail and sit down. North Wind will send you onwards. When you've crossed the river of Oceanus you will find a level shore and the woods of Persephone, tall birches and willows. Beach your ship and go to the dank House of Hades. That's where Pyriphlegethon, the 'river of fire', and Cocytus, the 'river of pain', run together, near Acheron, the 'river of sorrow', a branch of the Styx, the 'river of hate'. There's a rock just where Cocytus and Pyriphlegethon join. Get up close to the roaring rivers and dig a pit a forearm's length both ways. Pour an offering to the dead around the pit, first with milk, then honey, then wine, and finally with water. Sprinkle white barley around the pit. Then call out to the feeble heads of the dead, saying that when you get back to Ithaca you will sacrifice to them a barren young cow, the best that you have, and you'll load up the altar with offerings. And to Teiresias alone you will sacrifice separately a black ram, the finest in your flocks.

"When you have entreated the tribes of the dead, then kill a black ram and a black ewe, turning their heads towards Hades' House, while you face the streams of the river. Then many ghosts of the dead will come. Call to your men and tell them to skin and burn the sheep, and then pray to Hades and dread Persephone.

"Finally, draw your sword and sit by the pit. Do not allow the dead to come near the blood until you have questioned Teiresias. The oracle will come to you and will tell you where you need to go."

So she spoke, and at once it was dawn. She threw a tunic and cloak around me and dressed herself in a long white robe that she tied with a girdle of gold, and she placed a veil over her head. I went through her halls and roused my men.

"Get up, men, let us go! Circe has told me everything."

There was a man named Elpenor, the youngest in the crew, not much of a fighter and not too smart, who was lying on the roof of the house, wanting cool air because he was drunk. He heard the noise outside, jumped up and forgot the ladder. He fell headfirst from the roof. His neck was broken and his ghost went down to the House of Hades.

"Circe has told me we need to take another trip," I told my men. "It's to the House of Hades and Persephone, because we need a prophecy from the ghost of Theban Teiresias."

Their spirit was smashed within them. They wept and tore their hair. But it didn't do any good.

Book 11

HOUSE OF HADES

Odysseus held his listeners spellbound:

We reached the ship and dragged it into the bright sea. North Wind, sent by Circe, filled the sail and all day long we sped over the water. The sun set and the ways grew dark. We came to Oceanus, the deep-flowing stream that surrounds the Earth.

We beached the ship and walked until we came to the place that Circe had described. Here I dug a pit, then poured wine and sprinkled white barley. I prayed to the dead, then I cut the throats of the animals. The dark blood flowed into the pit.

Right away, ghosts crowded all around me: dead brides, handsome youths, worn-out old men, lively young girls not used to sorrow and the many who were wounded with bronze-tipped spears, killed in battle. They gathered round the pit and I was afraid! I called to my men and told them to skin and burn the sheep and to pray to Hades and Persephone. I sat by the pit with my sharp sword, but I would not allow the dead to come near the blood until I had questioned Teiresias.

The first ghost to arrive before me was Elpenor, whose corpse we had left unburied when we departed Circe's island. I wept when I saw him.

"Elpenor, how did this happen?" I asked. "You've come here faster on foot than we managed in our black ship!"

"I fell from the roof and broke my neck. Please burn me up with my armour and put a mound on my bones in memory of an unlucky man, and fix on the mound the oar I rowed with in life."

"All this, my unlucky comrade, I will do."

Then came the ghost of my dead mother, Anticlea, whom I'd left alive when I went to Troy. I wept when I saw her but still would not allow her to come near the blood.

Next came the ghost Teiresias, holding his golden staff.

"Son of Laertes, Odysseus of many wiles, most unlucky man. Why have you left the light of the sun and come to this place where there is no joy? Put away your sword so that I may drink of the blood and speak to you."

I stepped back and put my sword in its sheath as he bade me. When he had drunk the dark blood, the oracle said:

"You ask about your return, Odysseus, but a god will make this hard for you. You won't elude Poseidon's anger, because you blinded his son Polyphemus, the Cyclops. You will need to keep your spirit steady, and help your comrades do the same, when you come to the island of Thrinacia. You'll find cattle and sheep there that belong to the sun god, Helios. If you leave these alone you may reach Ithaca – but if you harm Helios' cattle then I foresee ruin. Only you shall escape, but you will come home late and in danger, having lost everything, and you will arrive in another man's ship. What's more, you'll find your house full of strife, arrogant men who consume your wealth and woo your wife and offer suitors' gifts.

"You will manage to take vengeance on them, but when you have killed the suitors you must leave again. You are to travel with an oar on your shoulder until you find men who know nothing of the sea and eat their food unmixed with salt – men who've never heard of ships or oars. When you meet a wayfarer who asks, "Is that a winnowing fan on your shoulder?" then fix your oar into the earth and make offerings to Lord Poseidon. Offer up a bull and a boar. Then go home and offer sacrifice to the gods who never die and live in heaven.

"And as for your own final end, a gentle death shall come to you far from the sea, when you are overcome with shining old age and your people dwell in richness around you. This is the truth."

"Teiresias, tell me, I see the ghost of my dead mother. Tell me, Teiresias, how may she recognize me?"

"Whichever of the dead you let come near the blood, that ghost will speak to you."

So saying, the ghost of Teiresias returned to the House of Hades. I remained motionless until my mother came up and drank the dark blood. At once she knew me.

"My child, how have you come beneath the murky darkness while still alive?" she cried aloud.

"Mother, I had to come down to the House of Hades to seek a prophecy from Theban Teiresias. But Mother, tell me, how did you die? And tell me about my father and the son I left behind. And what about my wife, what does she think? Does she stay with my son and keep everything safe?"

"Your wife remains steadfast in your house and each night she falls to weeping. Telemachus retains your lands. But your father stays out in the farmland and never comes to the town. He nurses his anguish and longs for your return.

"Sorrow overtook me, too, Odysseus. It was my longing for you and your advice, and for your kind heart, that robbed me of life."

I wanted to grasp the ghost of my dead mother and I sprang three times towards her and three times she flitted away like the shadow of a dream.

"Mother, why do you not stay for me when I want to hold you? Or are you a phantom that Persephone has sent so that I may groan still more?"

"Oh my child, most ill-fated of men. Persephone is not deceiving you. This is the way it is when you die. The sinews no longer hold flesh on the bones and the ghost flutters away like a dream."

Then other women came, the wives and daughters of famous men, sent by Persephone. One after the other they drew near and I questioned them.

The first woman was noble Tyro, the daughter of Salmoneus, the arrogant king who challenged Zeus. She fell in love with the river Enipeus, but Poseidon took on the form of Enipeus and had sex with Tyro. A black wave stood around them like a mountain, hiding the god and the woman. Afterwards, she fell asleep.

"As the year advances you will produce wonderful children," Poseidon told her, "for I am Poseidon, shaker of the earth."

He dived into the sea. She conceived and bore Peleus and Neleus, formidable followers of Zeus.

After that I saw Antiopê, who slept in the arms of Zeus and gave birth to twins, Amphion and Zethus, who built the walls of seven-gated Thebes. Then I saw Alkmenê, the wife of Amphitryon, mother of Heracles. And I saw the mother of Oedipus, beautiful Epicastê, who unknowing did a monstrous thing by marrying her own son. She went down to the House of Hades by attaching a strong noose from the ceiling. And I saw beautiful Chloris, queen of Pylos, who bore Nestor and many others.

And then I saw Leda, the wife of Tyndareus, who bore two sons, Castor, tamer of horses, and the boxer Polydeuces. They live one day in the world and one day in the House of Hades, honoured like gods. And I saw the beautiful Ariadnê, daughter of Minos, whom Theseus tried to bring to Athens, but Artemis killed her on Naxos when Dionysus told her to.

Then the ghost of Agamemnon came up to me. As soon as he drank the blood he knew me, and he cried aloud and shed tears. But he had lost his strength and power. I wept when I saw him.

"Glorious Agamemnon," I said, "how has death overcome you?"

"Odysseus, my cousin Aegisthus killed me with the help of my hateful wife. Aegisthus invited me to a feast at his house. You have witnessed many men killed in combat, but you would have felt pity if you had seen how blood swam around the tables laden with food. The saddest cry was from the daughter of Priam, my mistress Cassandra, a war captive. Clytemnestra killed her as she clung to me."

"Agamemnon, Zeus has tormented your family from the earliest days," I observed.

Agamemnon said, "You will not be a man who dies at the hand of his wife. The daughter of Icarius is a good woman. When we left, she had a boy, a baby. No doubt he is now a grown man. You, his father, will see him, and he will embrace you, as is right!"

So these were our sad exchanges, and we shed tears. Then the ghost of Achilles came to me, and the ghosts of Patroclus and of Ajax. Achilles recognized me.

"Son of Laertes, Odysseus, you stubborn man! What adventure greater than this will you ever contrive? How did you descend to Hades where the phantoms of men live?"

"Achilles, son of Peleus, I came here because I needed to talk to Teiresias and find out how to get back to Ithaca. No man was ever more blessed than you. When you were alive we honoured you like a god, and now that you are here you rule among the dead!"

"Don't glorify death, Odysseus. I would rather live as a peon without land than be king over the dead. But come, tell me of my son Neoptolemus. And let me hear about Peleus, my father – do the Myrmidons still honour him? If I could go with vigour to my father's house, just for an hour, I would make any man who served up violence to him rue the day."

"I've heard nothing of Peleus," I said, "but I can give you news of your son, Neoptolemus. I brought him from the island of Scyros to join the Achaean army. He was the best at giving counsel. Only Nestor and I were better. He never hung back when we fought on the Trojan plain, and he killed many in combat.

"And when we were about to get into the Trojan horse, and I was trying to get someone to open and close the door, the other Achaeans wiped tears from their eyes and their limbs shook, but I never once saw the handsome face of your son Neoptolemus grow pale. I never saw him wipe tears from his face. He asked me, "Let me open the horse!", eager to kill Trojans. After we sacked the city he went on board ship with his share of the loot and a noble prize – Andromachê, wife of Hector, whom he took as slave. He was unscathed, not wounded by the spear."

So I spoke, and the ghost of Achilles departed over the Fields of Asphodel, jubilant at hearing my news of his son.

And now the ghosts of other dead stood there, each asking about those dear to him. Ajax, son of Telamon, was still angry that I won the arms of Achilles. Achilles' mother, Thetis, set the arms out as a prize, and the judges were Trojan captives and, of course, Athena. I wish I'd never won that contest. Because of those arms, handsome Ajax was buried beneath a mound of earth. I spoke to Ajax with words I hoped would win his favour.

"Ajax, son of Telamon, will you not even in death forget your anger against me? We lost a tower of strength when we lost you, and we sorrowed unceasingly for you as much as for Achilles. No one else is to blame but Zeus. He hated the Achaean army and brought on your doom. Put aside your anger and your pride."

Ajax did not answer a word but went his way into the nether darkness.

I saw Minos, the son of Zeus, holding a golden sceptre, passing judgement on the dead.

And after Minos I became aware of the ghost of gigantic Orion hurrying over the fields; in his hands he held a bronze club.

And I saw Tityos, the son of Gaea. Two vultures sat on either side and tore at his liver, plunging their beaks into his guts, and he couldn't beat them off with his hands. For he raped Leto, the consort of Zeus, as she went towards Delphi.

Yes, and I saw Tantalus. He was standing in a pool of water that came up to his chin. He was crazy with a thirst that he could not quench, because when he stooped down to drink, the water was swallowed up by the earth so there was nothing there. And trees, high and leafy, let hang their fruit all around him – pears and pomegranates, bright apples, sweet figs and luscious olives. But as soon as the old man reached out to grab some, the wind blew them into the clouds.

Yes, and I saw another man in terrible suffering: Sisyphus, the brother of Salmoneus, who was trying to shift a gigantic stone with his two bare hands. He would push the stone to the top of the hill, but just before the crest it would roll back on itself, back down to the plain. He would strain again and try to push it up once more. The sweat flowed from his arms and his head.

And after him, I saw mighty Heracles – or rather, his phantom, for Heracles himself dines among the gods where he is married to Hebê, goddess of youth, a daughter of Zeus and Hera. All around Heracles' ghost a clamour arose from the dead, like the sound of chattering birds. He looked like dark night, poised with his bow out of its quiver, an arrow on the string. He glared fearsomely around him as if about to shoot. Across his chest was a bandelier of gold with wondrous animals fashioned in it: bears, wild boars, lions with sparkling eyes, fights, battles, murders, the killing of men.

"Son of Laertes, Odysseus," Heracles said, "you wretched man, do you suffer the same evil lot as I? I was the son of Zeus but I suffered immeasurable anguish. I was made to be a slave to a man far inferior. He sent me here once, to fetch the hound of Hades, for he couldn't think of a harder task. Hermes was my guide and Athena too."

So saying, Heracles went on his way, but I stood my ground, hoping that some other ghost might appear from the days of old. Perhaps I might have seen Theseus and Peirithoüs, marvellous offspring of the gods, but then the tribes of dead in their multitudes thronged around the pit. Terror seized me, and I feared that Persephone might send up the head of Gorgon, the abominable monster that turns you to stone.

Without waiting, I hurried down to the ship and told my men to loosen the cables and get us out of there. They went on board, sat down on the benches, and the ship was carried down the river Oceanus by the current. The wind blew us onwards.

Book 12

THE CATTLE OF THE SUN

Odysseus spoke on:

We headed back to Aeaea, the island of Circe. We beached our ship on the sands, went ashore and fell asleep. When dawn came, I sent men to Circe's house to retrieve Elpenor's corpse. We burned him and his armour where the headland juts out farthest to the sea. We heaped up a mound, put a marker on the tomb, and placed his well-made oar there too.

Circe came down to the shore, accompanied by her handmaid bringing bread, meat and wine.

"You've gone down alive to the House of Hades! Ordinary men die once, but you will meet death twice."

All day long, we feasted on meat and drink, and then when darkness came the men lay down to rest by the cables of the ship. Circe took me by the hand and led me a way apart from them.

"Now listen to what I tell you. First, you will sail past the two Sirens, who enchant all those who come their way. Around them are heaped the bones of rotting men, their skin all shrivelled. Seal the ears of your men with wax so that they cannot hear the Sirens' voices. If you want to listen to their song yourself, have your men tie you hand and foot on the mast. And if you beg them to release you, have them bind you tighter.

"Once past the Sirens, you must choose one of two directions. On one side there are crags projecting into the sea that are smashed constantly with waves. They're called the Planctae, or the Clashing Rocks. Not even winged creatures can get past, no, not even doves carrying food to Zeus.

The rocks always snatch one of them and Zeus has to send another to make up the number. Only one ship has ever passed the Planctae: the Argo, the most famous ship of all. It was on Jason's voyage to get the Golden Fleece, and the waves would have dashed even her against the rocks if Hera had not sent her through, because she so loved Jason.

"In the other direction, there are two cliffs. One reaches to the sky and is surrounded by a dark cloud. In the middle of the cliff is a dark cave. Inside is Scylla, an evil monster. She has twelve legs and six long necks, each with a terrifying head at the end of it. In each head are three rows of tightly packed teeth, ready for black death. Scylla holds her heads out over the chasm and searches for dolphins, maybe a whale, and whatever else she can catch. No ship has ever made it past Scylla unscathed, for with each of her six heads she carries off a man.

"The cliff opposite is close by. You could shoot an arrow across the gap. On this cliff there is a large fig tree, and beneath the tree, Charybdis sucks down the water. Three times a day she spits it up and three times she sucks it away. I hope you're not there when she gulps down the sea, because nobody could save you, not even Poseidon. Steer in close to Scylla's cliff, opposite Charybdis, and drive your ship past quickly. It's better to lose six of your men than all of them."

"Goddess, tell me," I said, "is there some way I can fight off Scylla when she tries to eat my men?"

"You wretch, all you think of is fighting!" Circe said. "Scylla's not mortal! She's a deathless evil, a terror. She's dreadful, ferocious, not to be fooled with. There is no defence against her. Fleeing is the best thing you can do.

"Next you will come to the island of Thrinacia. That is where the sun god Helios' livestock grazes, seven herds of cattle and seven of sheep, fifty in each. They do not bear young, nor do they die, and their shepherds are nymphs. If you leave the herds untouched, you may reach Ithaca. If you harm the herds of Helios, your ship is doomed, and your men, too."

So she spoke, and dawn rose. The goddess went up to her house and I went towards my ship and roused my men. They climbed on board. We stored the tackle in the ship, sat down on the benches and struck the sea with our oars. The wind and the helmsman guided us along. To help us, Circe sent a fair wind.

We came to the island of the Sirens. With my keen sword I cut a cake of wax and kneaded it in my hands. The wax softened and I placed some into each of my men's ears. They bound me to the mast and sat down at the benches and struck the water with their oars.

When we were shouting distance away, rowing fiercely, the Sirens started to sing.

"Come, renowned Odysseus, glory of the Achaeans! Stop so that your ship may hear our voices. Never yet has any man passed this island without hearing the sweet music from our lips. He feels the joy of it and he goes on his way, a wiser man."

Their voices were bewitching, and I told my comrades, "Let me go!" but they fastened on more ropes and drew them tightly together. When they had rowed past the Sirens and we could no longer hear their melody, my men removed the wax from their ears and untied me.

When we had put the island behind us, there was a great surge in the sea and I heard a booming. In their terror, the men stopped rowing. I made my way through the ship, bolstering each one in turn.

"My friends, we've experienced sorrow before, and the evil that comes on us now is no greater than when the Cyclops penned us in his cave. We escaped from there. Keep your seats on the benches and strike the sea with your oars in the hope that Zeus may help us avoid death!

"And you, helmsman, I give this command. Keep the ship far away from the great whirlpool and hug the opposite cliff. Otherwise you may swerve off into the vortex and cast us into destruction."

I didn't say anything about Scylla, a disaster we could not prevent.

I put on my armour and grasped two long spears. I went to the front of the ship to look out. My eyes grew tired as they gazed towards the murky rock.

We sailed up the narrow strait. On one side was Charybdis, gulping down the water. Whenever she belched it forth, she would seethe and bubble in chaos like a pot on a big fire, and high overhead the spray fell down on top of both cliffs. Every time she sucked down the water, you could see the earth appear, and my men were gripped by horror.

We looked towards Charybdis, fearing destruction, but as we did so, Scylla seized six men. Turning, I saw their feet and hands above me as they cried out, screaming my name. My men were raised up the cliffs squirming, as though a fisherman sitting on a jutting rock, casting his bait, had caught fish and then flung them writhing ashore. As I watched, Scylla ate my men in front of her cave as they shrieked, and they stretched out their hands towards me in their death struggle. This was the worst thing I ever saw at sea.

When we escaped the cliffs and the dread Scylla and Charybdis, we came to the island of Helios. I heard the lowing of cattle and sheep bleating. I remembered the words of Teiresias and Circe.

"Hear me, men, for all that you are suffering," I said. "Let me tell you what Teiresias and Circe said. They told me to keep away from the island of Helios, our greatest threat. Don't stop, row past this island!"

Their spirit was broken and Eurylochus answered with menacing words.

"You bastard, Odysseus! You must be made of iron, seeing how you won't allow your men, worn to death and sleep deprived, to set foot on shore where we might fix a meal. Let us rest in the evening and make dinner, staying close to the ship. We'll put out to sea in the morning."

The men agreed. I realized that some god was hatching evil plans!

"Eurylochus, you leave me with little choice, seeing I am alone in my views. All right, but swear a mighty oath. If we find a herd of cattle or flock of sheep, you will not kill one to eat."

They did swear, and we moored our ship near a spring of fresh water. The men got out and prepared their dinner. When they were full, they fell to weeping, remembering their comrades snatched by Scylla.

When it was well past midnight, Zeus stirred a savage wind. At dawn, with the gale still blowing, we dragged our ship up from the shore and tied it in a cave. I called my men together.

"My friends, in our ship is meat and drink. Let us keep our hands away from the cattle and the sheep of Helios, who sees all things."

They agreed. For an entire month, South Wind blew unceasingly. For as long as my men had grain and wine, they kept away from the livestock. When the stores were eaten, they had to roam around looking for game, fish and whatever else they might find, angling with bent hooks, for hunger pinched their bellies. Then I went further inland so I could pray to the gods. I washed my hands in a shelter and prayed. But all the gods did was to send sleep over my eyes.

In the meanwhile, Eurylochus gave out evil advice.

"Hear me, comrades in suffering. All forms of death are hateful but death from hunger is the worst. Let us take some of Helios' cattle and offer a sacrifice to the immortals. And if we ever get to Ithaca, we'll build a temple to Helios and make many offerings, and if Helios is still angry because of his cattle, well, I'd rather lose my life in one huge gulp of a wave than waste away on a desert island."

Right away my men drove off the best of the cattle – pretty animals with spiral horns. When they had prayed and sliced the throats of the cattle and skinned them, they cut out sections of the thighs, covered them in a double layer of fat and laid more raw meat on top. They didn't have wine to pour over the sacrifice, so they poured water instead. They roasted the guts over the fire. When the thigh pieces were burned and they had tasted the innards, they cut up the rest and roasted it on a spit.

Swiftly one of the nymphs who guard the flocks came to Helios and told him of the killing of his cattle.

"Father Zeus," the angry Helios said, "you must take vengeance on Odysseus' men. If they are not punished for murdering my cattle, I will go down to the House of Hades and shine among the dead!"

"Helios, keep shining among gods and mortal men," Zeus exclaimed. "As for Odysseus' men, I will hit their ship with a thunderbolt and shatter it in the wine-dark sea."

I later heard about this conversation from Calypso.

When I came down to the ship I scolded my men, but there was nothing to be done: the cattle were dead. Portents began to appear. The hides crawled on the ground, the meat groaned on the spits and there was the sound of cattle lowing.

For six days my comrades feasted on the cattle, but when on the seventh day the wind stopped, we went on board. We put up the mast and hoisted the sail. When we had left the island behind and no other land could be seen, Zeus set a black cloud above the ship and the sea grew dark. The shrieking West Wind started to blow furiously. The blast snapped the ropes of the mast so that it fell backwards and the tackle was strewn in the bilge. The mast hit the steersman and crushed the bones of his skull. Like a diver he plummeted from the deck. At the same time, Zeus thundered and hurled his lightning and the ship quivered from front to back. My men were pitched overboard and the waves carried them like sea crows, and the god took from them the day of their homecoming. Waves ripped the sides from the ship's keel. I lashed the mast and the keel together and sat astride them as they were swept along by the winds.

West Wind stopped blowing and South Wind came up. All night long I was carried over the seas, and when the sun rose I was back at Scylla's cliff and straight into Charybdis, who sucked down the sea water beneath me. I sprang to the fig tree at the top of the cliff above Charybdis and gripped it like a bat. There I clung until, to my joy, she spat up the mast and keel. I let go and fell into the water. Sitting once more astride the flotsam, I rowed with my hands. As for Scylla, she did not see me, or I would not have escaped.

For nine days and nights I was carried on the sea, and on the tenth the gods brought me to Ogygia, where Calypso lives.

Book 13

ITHACA AT LAST

The Phaeacians in the shadowy halls were spellbound as they listened in silence.

"Odysseus," Alcinoüs said finally, "I don't think you'll be wandering any more after having suffered so much. I speak now to every single person drinking this wine and listening to the singer. Stored in the chest there is clothing for the stranger, along with gold jewellery and the other gifts that you brought. But let us also give him a tripod and a cauldron. We will all contribute towards this!"

The Phaeacians agreed. Each man went home to sleep, and at dawn they hurried down to the ship, bringing a bronze tripod and cauldron. Alcinoüs himself stowed the gifts under the benches. Then Alcinoüs sacrificed a bull to Zeus. When they had burned the thigh pieces and eaten the meat, the minstrel Demodocus sang to his lyre. But Odysseus was impatient to be on his way. He was waiting for the sun to sink, the way a man who has ploughed all day with his oxen and longs for his dinner, knees aching with tiredness, is glad when the sun sets.

"Lord Alcinoüs, most famous of men, pour libations now and send me on my way. Your gifts will be a blessing in days to come, and I hope that on my return I will find my house in good order and my wife and my friends and family unharmed. And may you too be happy with your wives and children, and may the gods give you every good thing."

They praised his words. Alcinoüs said, "Mix up the wine in the bowl; let us pray to Father Zeus to take the stranger to his native land."

The wine was mixed and served and they poured libations. Then Odysseus stood up and placed in Queen Aretê's hand a two-handled cup.

"Farewell, my queen," he said, "may you be fortunate in all the years to come."

Alcinoüs sent a man to lead him down to the ship. Aretê sent three slave women, one holding a cloak and tunic, another carrying the treasure chest, and the third bringing bread and wine. When they reached the vessel, youths stowed everything away. Then they spread out a rug and blanket for Odysseus on the deck where he could sleep soundly. Odysseus lay down quietly. The Phaeacians sat on the benches. They leaned back and struck the brine with their oars as sleep overcame Odysseus, a sound sleep, a sweet sleep, a sleep like death.

Then the Phaeacian ship leapt high on the water, like four stallions yoked together springing up in unison under the lash, bounding across the plain. The resounding sea foamed in the ship's wake as she sped on her way.

Not even a hawk, the swiftest of birds, could have kept pace as she cut through the waves carrying a wise man who had suffered in war and on the sea. Now he slept in peace.

When the morning star appeared, heralding dawn, the Phaeacian ship drew near Ithaca. There is a harbour there of Phorcys, a god of the sea. At its mouth, two headlands project, each one sheer on the sea side but sloping on the harbour side. These headlands keep back the waves while beyond them ships lie unmoored. At the end of the harbour is an olive tree and near it a cave, the habitation of nymphs called Naiads. The bees store their honey there in mixing bowls and stone jars. There are looms made of stone where the Naiads weave purple fabrics, and inside the cave lie two springs that are always flowing.

They rowed into the harbour. The ship was speeding so fast that it ran up half its length onto the shore. The Phaeacians carried Odysseus out of the ship and laid him on the sand, where he lay still overpowered by sleep. They took out the treasures and set them near the trunk of the olive tree, away from the path so a stranger would not steal them. Then they turned round to go home.

But Poseidon did not forget the threats he had made against Odysseus. He spoke to Zeus:

"Father Zeus, I shall not be honoured among the gods when even mortals don't respect me, not even the Phaeacians who are my descendants! I declared that Odysseus would suffer before he got home, though I did not rob him of his homecoming altogether, because you had promised he would have it. Yet these men have carried him asleep in a swift ship over the sea and set him down in Ithaca, and they've given him gifts: bronze, gold, woven cloth – more than he would have won from Troy if he had returned unscathed."

"Lord Poseidon, what are you saying?" Zeus answered. "The gods don't dishonour you, our eldest and best sibling. The Phaeacians will be

watching from their city as the ship sails in. Turn the vessel to stone as they look out, so that all men may marvel at the sight! And then hide their city behind a mountain."

When Poseidon heard this, he went off to Scheria, the island of the Phaeacians. As the ship came into shore he turned it into stone with a blow from the palm of his hand.

The Phaeacians were amazed. "Who has bound our ship on the sea as she came in?"

Alcinoüs addressed them. "It's true that my father, who consulted many oracles, told me that one day a ship returning from convoy would turn to stone and that we would be encircled by a mountain. We must sacrifice twelve bulls to Poseidon and hope that he pities us."

In terror they made ready the bulls for sacrifice.

Odysseus awoke in his native land. He did not recognize anything. Athena shed a mist around him so that nobody would realize who he was, until the suitors had paid the price for their acts.

But all the surroundings seemed unfamiliar to their ruler: the paths, the bays, the cliffs, the luxurious trees. Odysseus looked at his native land and groaned. He slapped his thighs with the flats of his hands. "Alas, where have I come? I wish I'd stayed among the Phaeacians. Now I don't know where to put this treasure. I cannot leave it here, in case somebody steals it. The Phaeacians have not done right by me, coming to a strange land. They said they'd bring me to Ithaca but they haven't kept their word."

Then Athena came near him. She took on the form of a young man, a herdsman. She wore a cloak in a double fold about her shoulders, and sandals beneath her feet. In her hands she held a spear.

"My friend, you are the first I've seen in this land!" Odysseus said when she approached. "May you wish me well and save this treasure I have, and save me, too! I come to you as if to a god, a suppliant at your knees. Tell me: what place is this? Who lives here?"

"You're a fool, sir, or else you've come from far away. This land is not nameless. It's a rugged island, not good for horses, but not completely poor, although small. Grain grows here and grapes for wine, and the rain falls, and in the morning there is dew. It is ideal for goats and cattle. Trees are plentiful and there are many springs that always flow. The name of Ithaca has reached even the land of Troy, which they say is a long way away."

Odysseus rejoiced when he heard Athena say this. He replied, but without revealing the truth, for he was a cunning thinker.

"Indeed, I have heard of Ithaca even in Crete, which is far over the sea. I have come here by myself with my goods. I killed the son of Idomeneus, Orsilochus, the fastest runner in Crete. Orsilochus wanted to rob me of the booty I took from Troy, for which I suffered much, because I would not serve as his underling in the land of the Trojans. I could not, for I had men under my own command. So I struck Orsilochus with my spear one night as he came back from the fields. I lay in wait by the roadside with one of my men. It was dark and nobody saw us. I took his life unseen.

"I immediately ran to the shore and begged for help from some Phoenicians there, giving them plenty of booty in return. I told them to take me aboard and deposit me at Pylos or nearby, but the wind drove them here. They did not mean to play me false but were beaten back in this direction, so we arrived at night. We rowed into the harbour, disembarked, and I was so tired I lay straight down and fell asleep. They brought me my belongings while I lay dreaming on the sands."

Athena smiled and stroked Odysseus with her hand and changed into the form of a woman – beautiful, tall, expert in fine handiwork – and said:

"Even a god would have to be cunning indeed to surpass your trickery! You are a stubborn man! Not even in your own land, which you love from the bottom of your heart, do you abandon your deceitful ways. Come, let us not talk of this further. You are the best at clever speech, but I am famous among the gods for my knowledge and my craftsmanship.

"Do you not know me? I am Athena, the daughter of Zeus, who's always protected you throughout your troubles. I made you beloved by the Phaeacians, and now I've come to concoct a plan with you, hide the treasure and tell you of the strife you will find in your house. You will need to be strong . . . You must cope with what's to come. Don't tell any man or woman you are back, but submit to the violence of those interlopers in silence."

"It's hard, goddess, for a mortal man to know you when he meets you, however wise he is," Odysseus said, "for you take on any form you want. But I well know that you were on my side throughout our time in Troy. Then after we sacked the city of Priam and left in our ships, the gods scattered the Achaeans. I never saw you then at sea. When I was with the Phaeacians you cheered me with your words and you yourself led me to their city. And now I must ask you, by your father, surely this cannot be Ithaca? No, surely it's some other place, and you mock me. Tell me: have I truly arrived in Ithaca, my native land?"

"I cannot leave you in despair! You're discreet and smart and careful. Another man returning from his wanderings would hurry to his house to see his children and wife. She passes her days and nights weeping. I was sure that you would make it home after losing all your men, but you must understand that when you were at sea I was unwilling to go against Lord Poseidon, my father's brother, angry because you blinded his son Polyphemus, the Cyclops. Let me show you now that yes, this is your own island.

"This is the harbour of Phorcys, a god of the sea, and here is the olive tree at its head, and here is the cave where nymphs live, the Naiads. You used to make offerings to the Naiads in that cave. Over there is Mount Neriton, covered in forest."

She dispersed the mist and suddenly he saw the land she pointed to. He rejoiced and prayed to the Naiads in the cave with outstretched hands. "I never thought I'd see you again," he said to them, "but I pray to you now, with loving prayers. I'll offer you gifts as I used to do, if Athena grants that I live."

"Be cheerful, Odysseus; don't be sad," Athena said. "Let us stow your treasures in the cave where they will stay safe. Then we can think about things."

The goddess went into the cave and looked for hiding places. Odysseus took the goods inside and Athena blocked the opening with a stone.

Then the two sat down by the olive tree and plotted death for the men who had been insulting Odysseus' wife.

"Odysseus, consider how to attack the suitors who for three years have taken over your halls, courting Penelope."

"I was about to be killed in my own house," Odysseus said, emphatically, "just like Agamemnon, if you had you not told me everything. But let us plan how I can defeat them. Stand by me and give me courage, the kind I had when we sacked Troy. If you'd be there for me, goddess, I'd fight three hundred men!"

"I will be with you and I will not forget you, and the men who consume your property will spatter the earth with their blood and brains. But come, I will make you unknown to everybody. I'll shrivel your handsome skin and ruin your fair hair and clothe you in a way anyone would shudder to see. I will dim your eyes, so beautiful before, to make you ugly in the suitors' sight and in the sight of your wife and son, too.

"First, go to see the swineherd who keeps your pigs. He likes you and he loves Telemachus and Penelope. You'll find him by the Rock of the Crows and the Spring of Arethusa, where the pigs grow fat on acorns and drink the water. Stay there and question him while I visit Sparta to find your son Telemachus, who travelled to the palace of Menelaüs to discover whether you were still alive."

"Why didn't you just tell him? Was that so that he could suffer, wandering over the seas?"

"Don't worry about him. I guided him. He will earn a good reputation and he's not in trouble. He's living peacefully in Menelaüs' palace. True, the insolent suitors lie in wait for him, eager to kill him when he comes

back, but I don't believe they will succeed. The men who devour your wealth will be covered in earth before then!"

So saying, Athena touched Odysseus with her wand. She withered the flesh on his limbs and destroyed his hair and she put the skin of an aged old man on his limbs. She dimmed his eyes and dressed him in a ragged cloak and tunic – tattered clothes fouled and begrimed with filthy smoke. Around his shoulders she put the skin of a deer stripped of its hair, and she gave him a staff and a wretched leather pouch full of holes, with a strap of twisted cord.

Their plans made, the two of them parted. The goddess went to Sparta to fetch the son of Odysseus.

Book 14

FEAST OF THE
DISGUISED STRANGER

Odysseus followed the rugged path up from the harbour to the place where Athena had told him the swineherd, Eumaeus, would be. He found him sitting in front of his hut. Nearby was a courtyard, built on a high spot with sweeping views and open space all around. The swineherd had built the walls of the yard himself, using enormous stones, and topped them with a cap of thorn bushes. He had driven huge stakes along the walls that he made by splitting oak trees to their black core. Within the courtyard he'd constructed twelve sties for the swine; each one held fifty females. The boars slept outside the yard. They were far fewer in number because the insolent suitors had been feasting on them; three hundred and sixty remained. Next to the boars slept four dogs – savage, wild! – that the swineherd had raised.

The dogs noticed Odysseus and rushed at him, barking loudly. He would have been cruelly attacked – even though he was in his own farmyard – but Eumaeus came after the hounds, shouting and scattering them.

"Old man!" he called. "The dogs might have torn you to shreds! And the gods would have given me yet more grief. I am grieving anyway for my master as I rear these fat swine for other men to eat. But let's go to my hut, old man, and you can eat and drink and tell me your sufferings."

Eumaeus led Odysseus to his hut. He sat him on his bed of brushwood, spread with the shaggy skin of a wild goat.

Odysseus said: "Stranger, may Zeus and the other immortals give you what you want most, because you have made me welcome."

"Well, it's not right to turn away a stranger, even he is of less account. Strangers and beggars are from Zeus, and I welcome you with gifts, however small. Life is precarious for slaves like me. My master would have taken care of me if he had grown old here in the house."

Eumaeus went out to the sties. He selected two pigs to kill, then singed the meat and cut it up, putting it on spits. When the meat was roasted he set it before Odysseus, sprinkling it with white barley. He mixed wine in a bowl of ivy wood and sat down opposite his guest.

"Eat now, stranger, such food as slaves have to offer, the meat of young pigs. The suitors eat the fatted hogs. They have no pity. The gods abhor such behaviour! My master's property was great once. No one else, not even twenty men together, had such riches. I tell you – twelve herds of cattle on the mainland, and as many flocks of sheep again, and droves of swine, and herds of goats. And here too on Ithaca he has eleven herds of goats. But day after day the herdsmen must give the best animals to the suitors."

Odysseus gratefully ate the meat and drank the wine, and ruminated darkly on the suitors' deaths.

"My friend, who was your master?" Odysseus asked. "He must have been rich and powerful. Tell me, I might know him, for I've wandered far."

"Old man," answered Eumaeus, "wanderers wanting a handout tell all kinds of lies. Often a traveller goes up to the house and tells my mistress a tale of her husband. She receives him with kindness and tears fall from her eyes. And I think you too, old man, would make up some story in return for a cloak and a garment.

"As for my master, dogs and birds have torn off the skin from his bones and his spirit has fled, or maybe the fish in the sea ate him, and his bones lie on some shore buried in sand. Never again will I find a master so kind. My longing for him crushes me. He loved me and cared for me."

"My friend," Odysseus replied, "I tell you that Odysseus *will* return. And when he does, you can give me a cloak and tunic. I won't take anything before then. So be my witness, Zeus and all the other gods, that these things shall come to pass. This very month Odysseus will be back. He will return and take revenge on those who dishonour his wife and his son."

"Old man, I shall certainly not be paying you this reward, for Odysseus will never return to his house!" Eumaeus replied. "My heart is torn when anyone mentions my master. It's his son I worry about. He went off to Pylos looking for news. And now, I have heard, suitors lie in wait to attack him on his homeward journey, so the house of Odysseus may perish.

"But you, old man, tell me of your troubles. Who are you? Where do you come from? What is your city? Where are your parents? On what ship did you get here?"

"I will tell you," Odysseus answered. "I come from Crete, the son of a rich man. He had other sons too from a lawful wife, but my mother was a concubine. My father's name was Castor, son of Hylax, who honoured me as a trueborn son. He had high standing among the Cretans. But death carried him to the House of Hades and his sons divided up the property. They gave me a very small plot of land.

"I took a rich wife because I was prized for my strength and bravery. In those days Ares and Athena gave me the courage to break battle lines, and with my proud spirit I never feared death. I was always the first to rush forwards and kill the enemy. Before the Achaeans set foot at Troy, I had nine times led fighters and ships, and I amassed enormous spoils.

"When the time came for the expedition to Troy, the Cretans ordered me and Lord Idomeneus to lead their ships. For nine years the Achaeans warred in Troy and in the tenth year we sacked the city of Priam. We set out for home, but Zeus had evil plans for me. I made it to Crete and stayed for one month, rejoicing in my children and wife and in my riches, and then I set out for Egypt with my comrades.

"North Wind blew fair and we glided onwards as if sailing downstream. On the fifth day, we came to Egypt. I moored my ships in the river Aegyptus and told my men to guard them while I sent out scouts. But in their arrogance my men laid waste to the fields and carried off the women and children and killed the men. The cry quickly went up all through the city. Everybody heard the shouting, and at dawn they all emerged and the plain was filled with soldiers and chariots and the flashing of bronze.

"Zeus cast a thunderbolt on my men and not one had the courage to hold his ground. Danger surrounded us. Many were killed with bronze weapons and others were led to the city as slaves. I am sorry that I didn't die there, so much torment was to come. I took off my helmet, threw away my shield, put down my spear and ran to the chariot of the king. I seized his knees and kissed him. He pitied me and put me in his vehicle and he took me, weeping, to his home. An angry mob rushed forwards eager to kill me, but the king restrained them. He respected Zeus' anger, the god of strangers who punishes evil done to them.

"I stayed there for seven years. In the eighth year a man arrived from Phoenicia, a greedy cheat. He prevailed on me to go back with him to his land. He forced me on a ship bound for Libya, to sell me as a slave.

"The ship was sailing out on a course south of Crete, propelled by North Wind, but Zeus set a dark cloud over us and the sea grew black. The god thundered and hurled his lightning bolt, and the ship quivered from stem to stern and was filled with sulphur. The crew fell overboard, landing on the waves like sea crows.

"As for me, in this desperate moment, Zeus himself placed in my hand the mast of the ship. I clung to it and was swept along by the winds. For nine days I was carried over the sea, but on the tenth I came to the land of the Thesprotians. There the king took me in.

"That's where I learned about Odysseus. The king said that he had entertained him and welcomed him on his way to Ithaca, and he showed me the treasure that Odysseus had gathered – bronze and gold and carefully worked iron. It would feed his children for ten generations, so great was the wealth stored up for him.

"He said that Odysseus had gone on a visit to Dodona to consult an oracle from Zeus, the oak tree there, about how he should return to Ithaca. A Thesprotian ship happened to be headed for Dulichium where I wanted to go. He told them to take me to the king there; but instead they hatched an evil plan.

"When the ship was a good way from land, they plotted to sell me into slavery. They took off my clothes, and they dressed me in this torn shirt. When it got dark, they reached Ithaca. They bound me with a rope, leaving me on the ship while they went ashore for dinner. The gods themselves untied the rope and I slid down the loading plank and swam to shore. I went into a thicket and lay down, cowering. The gods hid me and now have led me to the farmstead of a wise man, you, Eumaeus. It appears I'm going to live."

"Ah, poor stranger, you've moved me with your tales of suffering on your travels. But you've not spoken truly about one thing: you'll never persuade me to believe your story about Odysseus. I know that the gods must have hated my master because they did not kill him among the Trojans, with his friends. If they had, the Achaeans could have made him a fitting tomb and he would have been bathed in glory. But instead, stormy seas have carried him away without honour.

"For my part, I simply live here with the pigs, and I don't go to the city unless Penelope asks me to when she hears some news. I don't bother to ask any questions, not since the time a man lied to me, a man on the run for murder, who came to my house. I welcomed him and he said he'd seen Odysseus among the Cretans at the house of Idomeneus, fixing his ships ruined in a storm. He said that Odysseus would be here by summer, or maybe by autumn, bringing piles of treasure and accompanied by his men. But he didn't come

"I can see that you're a man who has suffered much, but don't try to curry favour by lying to me. I respect you out of honour for Zeus, the stranger's god, not because of the tales you tell."

"You just don't want to believe me," Odysseus answered, "even though I've sworn an oath. But let's make a deal, and the gods will be our witness. If your master does come back to his house, then give me a cloak and a tunic to wear and send me to Dulichium, the place I am trying to reach. But if your master never comes, set the slaves on me and throw me from a cliff so that the next beggar will think twice about telling lies!"

"Truly that would make me famous among men now and for ever, if I brought you to my house, entertained you and then killed you! And how then could I ever pray in good faith to Zeus? It's time for food now. My fellow workers will soon be here; we can prepare a good dinner in the hut."

The swineherds arrived back. They shut up the sows and noisy grunting filled the sties. One of the herdsmen called to his fellow slaves. "Bring out

the best boar and we'll kill him for this stranger, and we will benefit too, we who toil caring for swine that others eat up."

Eumaeus split some wood and the other slaves brought a five-year-old boar up to the fireplace. The swineherd did not forget the gods; as a first offering he threw bristles from the boar's head into the fire and he prayed that Odysseus might come back. Then Eumaeus struck the boar with a club. The other slaves cut the boar's throat and singed the meat and then cut it up. The swineherd took pieces of flesh, laid them in rich fat and threw these into the fire after sprinkling them with barley. They sliced up the rest, spitted it, roasted it, drew off the spits and placed the meat on platters. Eumaeus carved it into seven pieces. He set one piece aside for the nymphs and Hermes and the rest he gave to his fellow slaves. He gave Odysseus a long piece from the backbone.

"Eumaeus, may Zeus love you as I love you, since, wretched though I am, you give me the best portion of meat."

"Enjoy the food," Eumaeus answered. "The god gives one thing and takes away another, as he pleases."

He put a small portion of his meat in the fire as an offering and he poured out an offering of wine, then he put the cup in Odysseus' hands and sat down.

Then Odysseus decided to test Eumaeus even further.

"Hear me now, Eumaeus, and the rest of you! I'll tell a boastful tale. The wine urges me on, heady drink that prompts even wise men to sing and laugh.

"I wish I were young again and as strong as I was when we readied an ambush under the walls of Troy. The leaders of the ambush were Odysseus and Menelaüs and I was third in command. When we came to the city wall we hid in the brush and the swamp, crouching down. Bitter night came on. North Wind dropped away and the frost came, then a covering of snow, and ice formed on our shields. The rest of the men had cloaks and tunics and were sleeping, their shields covering their shoulders, but when I set out I'd left my cloak behind thinking it would not be so cold, and so I had only my shield and my metal belt. When it was late at night and the stars had turned, I spoke to Odysseus, who was close by.

"'Odysseus,' I said, 'son of Laertes, I have to tell you that I won't be long among the living. I'm dying of the cold. I have no cloak. Some god fooled me into wearing just my tunic and now there is no escape.'

"Odysseus came up with a plan. He was great at schemes and at fighting and speaking. 'Be quiet now so none of the men will hear you,' he whispered. Then he propped himself up on his elbow and spoke loudly. 'Hear me, my friends, I had a dream from the gods while I was sleeping. We have come too far from the ships. I wish that someone would go and give word to Agamemnon so that he can send more men to join us.'

"So he spoke, and one of the men jumped up and threw down his cloak and set off at a run to the ships. Then I lay in his cloak and Dawn appeared on her golden throne. I wish I were young now as I was then, and one of you swineherds would give me a cloak out of kindness and respect."

"Old man you've told us a good tale," Eumaeus said, "and you've not said anything amiss since you've been here. So you won't lack clothing or anything else, but you'll receive what is appropriate for a suppliant. For tonight, at least, you'll have a cloak, but in the morning you'll have to manage with those rags of yours. We don't have extra cloaks here or changes of garments; every man has but the one."

Eumaeus stood up and made a bed for Odysseus near the fire, covering it with the skins of sheep and goats. Odysseus lay down and the swineherd threw over him a thick cloak that he kept to keep him dry when a heavy storm arose.

Odysseus slept beside the swineherd and his men. But Eumaeus was not happy to lie down away from his boars. He put his sharp sword over his shoulder. Then he gathered around himself a cloak to keep off the wind and he picked up the fleece of a large goat. He took a spear as protection against dogs and men and went outside to lie down with the white-tusked boars beneath a cavern in the rock, in a place sheltered from North Wind.

Book 15

EUMAEUS
THE SWINEHERD

Meanwhile, Athena went to Sparta to ensure Telemachus' return to Ithaca. She found him and Pisistratus, son of Nestor, in Menelaüs' glorious palace. Telemachus was unable to sleep. Athena stood next to him and said,

"Telemachus, you must not spend so much time away from home. Rouse Menelaüs now and ask him to send you on your way. The suitors are lying in wait in the strait between Ithaca and Cephalonia. They intend to kill you before you reach land. But I don't believe they will succeed.

"Keep your ship well away from the islands and travel by night. One of the immortals who watch over you will send a fair wind. When you reach Ithaca, beach your ship and direct your men towards the city, but you go straight to the hut of the swineherd."

Athena went off to Olympus. Telemachus woke up Pisistratus. "Get up! Fetch your horses! Yoke them to the chariot and let's get going!"

"Telemachus, we can't drive through darkness. Just hang on. Dawn will rise soon, and King Menelaüs will bring gifts and send us on our way."

Soon dawn appeared. Menelaüs got up from his bed where he lay with the beautiful Helen. When Telemachus saw him, he hurried to put on his tunic and cloak and went to speak to him.

"Menelaüs, son of Atreus, send me back now to my native land, for I must hurry home."

"Telemachus, I shall not be one who holds you back. A good host should welcome his guest, and then see him off when he wants to leave!

"Wait a moment, and I'll bring you some presents and put them in your chariot. And I'll tell the women to prepare a meal. If you wish to travel across the country, then I can go with you. I'll take you to all the cities! No one will send us away empty handed – everybody will give us gifts."

"Menelaüs, son of Atreus, I'd rather go home right away. I'm afraid that in looking for my father I may meet my end, or that his valuables will be stolen from his house."

When Menelaüs heard this, he at once told his wife Helen and her handmaids to prepare a meal. Then he went down to his treasure chamber, accompanied both by Helen and their son Megapenthes. Menelaüs took up a two-handled cup and he asked Megapenthes to bring the mixing bowl of silver. Helen went to the chest full of embroidered robes, some of which she had made herself, and took out the grandest dress, which shone like a star. They went back to Telemachus with these riches.

"Telemachus, may Zeus grant all you desire! Of all the treasures I have, I will give you the most beautiful and precious of all, a mixing bowl, entirely silver with a gold rim. It was made by Hephaestus and given to me by the king of the Sidonians in Asia, a Phoenician."

Strong Megapenthes brought up the mixing bowl and set it down in front of Odysseus. Menelaüs placed the two-handled cup into Telemachus' hands. Helen gave him the precious robe.

"I give you this gift too, my child," she said, "so that you will remember Helen on your wedding day. It's for your bride to wear. Until then, entrust it to your mother's care. And I wish you and your household every joy in your native land."

She put the robe in his hands and he took it gladly. Pisistratus placed the gifts in the chariot. He gazed in wonder at their splendour. Then Menelaüs led them into the halls and they sat down on chairs. A handmaid brought water in a pitcher of gold and poured it over a silver basin to rinse their hands while the housemaid drew up tables and laid out bread and meat. Megapenthes poured the wine.

So they set to breakfast with good cheer, and when they had satisfied their hunger, Telemachus and Pisistratus yoked the horses and climbed into the chariot. They walked the horses out of the gate and Menelaüs followed, holding wine in a cup of gold so they could offer libations.

"Farewell then, my good young men, and pass on my very best regards to Nestor. He was like a father to me when we Achaeans warred at Troy."

"We will of course give him your message," Telemachus said. "And I hope that when I return to Ithaca I find Odysseus in his house, and I can tell him how I received every kindness from you."

As he spoke these words, an eagle flew by on his right-hand side carrying a huge white goose that it had snatched from the yard; a crowd of women followed, shouting. The eagle swooped near and then darted off in front of the horses. Everyone was glad when they saw this omen.

"Was this for you, Menelaüs, or for us that the gods showed this sign?" Pisistratus asked.

Helen spoke before Menelaüs could answer. "Listen, and I will explain. Just as the eagle comes from the mountains, and has snatched a goose who lives in the house, so shall Odysseus return and take vengeance on the men who court his wife."

"May Zeus grant this," said Telemachus.

Pisistratus touched the horses with the lash. They streaked through the city. All day long they strained at the yoke and soon they reached Pylos.

"Make me a promise, my friend, and do as I say," Telemachus said to Pisistratus. "We're old friends because of our fathers' friendship and our similar ages, and this journey has brought us together. Leave me at my ship. Don't take me to Pylos, because I fear that your father Nestor will detain me in his house, but I need to get home."

Pisistratus turned his horses towards the ship. When they arrived, he took out the beautiful gifts that Menelaüs had supplied and put them in the stern. Then Pisistratus drove his horses back to Pylos. Telemachus joined his men.

"Get the tackle into the boat, my friends, and let us get on our way."

His men sat down on the benches. Telemachus killed an animal in Athena's honour, standing by the stern. While he was praying, a stranger came up to him. He was fleeing from Argos because he had killed a man. He was an oracle named Theoclymenus, descended from a long line of seers.

"My friend," Theoclymenus said to Telemachus, "I ask you, by the god to whom you pray, and also by your own life and the lives of your men: who are you? And from where? Where is your city, and who are your parents?"

"Stranger, I'm from Ithaca. My father is Odysseus, if he still lives. I'm trying to get news of him; he has been gone so long."

"I too left my own country, because I killed a man, one of my cousins. And now his brothers and other cousins want to kill me. I'm fleeing for my life. Take me onto your ship since I asked while you were praying. They will kill me otherwise, and they're right behind me."

"I would never drive you away! Come with us."

He took Theoclymenus' spear and laid it on the deck then climbed on board himself. Telemachus sat in the stern with Theoclymenus beside him. His men loosened the cables and set up the mast in its hollow socket. They tied it down with ropes and hoisted the sail held by twisted thongs of ox hide. Athena sent them a fair wind. The sun set and the waves grew dark. The ship sailed past the mainland and turned towards home.

On Ithaca, Odysseus and Eumaeus were having supper in the hut. When they had satisfied their hunger, Odysseus tested the swineherd, to see if he would continue to host him, or whether he'd pack him off to the city.

"Listen, Eumaeus, and you men, in the morning I'm thinking of going to the city to beg, as that way I won't ruin you with my needs. Perhaps you can give me some advice. Someone might offer me a cup of water and a piece of bread. I might even go to Odysseus' house and bear tidings to Penelope and enjoy the company of the suitors, to see whether they'd give me any dinner. I could serve them in any way they need. I am tremendous at serving. No other man can equal me in making a fire, splitting wood, carving and roasting meat, or in pouring wine."

"Why has such a thought come into your mind?" asked Eumaeus, deeply moved. "You must have a death wish to want to mingle with the throng of suitors whose debauchery and violence know no limits! Their serving men are young with fine clothes. They have handsome faces; they're slick. No, stay here! You're not bothering anybody, not me, not the others. And when Odysseus' son arrives he will give you a cloak and tunic, and he will send you wherever you want to go."

"Eumaeus, I hope that Zeus will love you as I do. You have put an end to my wandering. Homelessness is the worst thing for a mortal. Since you keep me here and urge me to await your master's return, tell me about the mother of Odysseus, and his father too. When he went to war he left his father behind on the verge of old age, I think. Are his parents still alive? Or are they dead and in the house of Hades?"

"Laertes is still alive but he grieves terribly for his son who is gone, and for his wife, whose death has made him old before his time. She wasted away from grief for her son. She brought me up with Ctimenê, Odysseus' sister, her youngest child. She cared for me as if I were her own. They sent Ctimenê to Cephalonia, the big island across the channel, to marry Eurylochus, one of Odysseus' followers. The family received countless bridal gifts! As for me, my lady Anticlea, Odysseus' mother, gave me fresh clothes and sandals and sent me to the fields."

"You must have been young when you were taken from your country," said Odysseus. "Tell me: was a city sacked where your father and mother lived? Or were you alone with your sheep and cattle when men took you for sale?"

"Stranger, since you ask, sit quietly while I speak. There's a time to sleep and a time to enjoy listening to stories. If any of the other men wish, they can go outside now and take a rest. In here, for the moment, we will drink and have a good time, enjoying hearing each other's tales of woe. Eventually a man finds pleasure even in pain, if he has suffered much and wandered much.

"There's an island called Syria, if you've heard of it. It's above Ortygia, where the sun turns. It's not densely settled but it's a good place. There are plenty of herds and flocks, lots of wine, much wheat. Famine never comes; nor does anybody ever get sick. When men grow old in the city, Artemis and Apollo with his silver bow take them with gentle shafts and they die. There are two cities on the island and all the land is divided between them. A king ruled over both: my father, Ctesius, a man like the gods.

"One day greedy Phoenicians arrived bringing all kinds of trinkets. In my father's house was a Phoenician woman, lovely looking and skilled in handiwork. The Phoenicians charmed her as she was washing clothes. They asked her where she came from and she showed them my father's house.

"'I come from Sidon,' she said, 'rich in bronze. I am the daughter of Arybas who was very wealthy. But Taphian pirates seized me when I was coming home from the fields and brought me here and sold me.'

"'Why don't you come with us to your home so you may see the house of your father and mother, and see them too?' asked the man. 'They're still alive and they're very rich.'

"'Perhaps I will,' the woman answered, 'if you swear an oath that you will take me to my home in safety.'

"They did swear. Then the woman said: 'Be quiet now and don't let anyone from your company speak to me if we meet in the street or at the well. I'm afraid that someone may go to the palace and tell the king so that he becomes suspicious and ties me up and plots to kill you. Pay attention. As soon as you can, barter your wares. When your ship is filled, send a messenger to me at the palace. I will bring whatever gold I can get – and something else, too. My master, the king, has a noble child. I am his nurse. The child is very intelligent. He goes with me when I go out. I can bring him on board and you would get a big price for him wherever you might sell him.'

"So saying, she went up to the palace. The Phoenicians remained there a whole year and acquired a lot of property by trade. When the ship was full to the brim for their return, they sent a messenger to the woman. A man came into my father's house, a highly skilled trickster. He brought a necklace made of gold and amber beads. All the women and my mother were handling the necklace and looking at it and offering him a price. He nodded silently to my nurse, then went to his ship. She led me by the hand out of my father's house. In the porch of the palace she scooped up cups from the banqueters' tables. She hid three goblets in her clothing and I followed innocently.

"The sun set and the ways grew dark as we hurried to the harbour and the Phoenician ship. Both of us climbed on board. We sailed over the waters and Zeus sent a fair wind. For six days we sailed, but when the seventh came,

Artemis struck my nurse and she fell with a clunk into the bottom of the boat, the way an osprey plunges into the sea. The Phoenicians threw her overboard to be eaten by seals and fishes, and I was left distraught.

"The wind and the waves brought them to Ithaca and here Laertes bought me with his riches. This is how I first saw this land."

"Eumaeus, you've moved me deeply with your tale of your suffering. Yet Zeus has granted you good things along with the bad, because after all your troubles you've come to the house of an upright man who gives you food and drink, who treats you kindly, and you live well. As for me, I wandered through the cities of many men before I reached this place."

So they swapped tales, then they lay down to sleep – but not for long, as dawn soon came.

Now Telemachus' boat drew near the shore. His men furled the sail and took down the mast. They rowed the boat to an anchorage, threw out the mooring stones and fixed the ropes at the rear of the boat. They then got out and prepared a meal.

"You men, row the boat towards the city," Telemachus said after they had finished eating. "I want to visit our lands and talk to the herdsmen. I'll come into the city once I've looked everything over."

"But where shall I go, dear child?" Theoclymenus asked. "Should I go straight to your mother's house and your house?"

"Ordinarily I would recommend you go up to our house. But I won't be there, and Mother will probably not see you. She doesn't appear often, preferring to stay apart and weave at her loom. But there's another man you can go with: he's named Peiraeus."

Just as Telemachus spoke, a bird flew by on the right-hand side, a hawk, messenger of Apollo. In its talons it held a dove that it plucked, shedding feathers on the ground between the ship and Telemachus.

Theoclymenus called Telemachus apart from his men and held his hand. "I don't think this bird flew by on our right without a god's urging.

I knew when I saw it that it was an omen. There is no race more kingly than yours among the people of Ithaca, and your race will be mighty."

"Stranger, I hope your words come true. Then you will receive great friendship and generosity from me." Telemachus turned to one of his men. "Peiraeus, you are most faithful to me of all my men who went to Pylos, so I ask you to take this man to your house and honour him until I get back."

"No matter how long you stay here," Peiraeus replied, "I'll entertain him and he will not lack what is owed to strangers."

Peiraeus returned on board the ship and told his comrades to loosen the ropes. He and Theoclymenus sat down. The men shoved the boat off and sailed to the city as Telemachus had instructed.

Telemachus walked hastily to the farmstead where his swine were kept. The swineherd slept among them, always loyal to his master.

Book 16

FATHER AND SON

In the swineherd's hut, Odysseus and Eumaeus were preparing breakfast. Eumaeus sent the other slaves out to take care of the pigs. As Telemachus approached the hut, the dogs fawned on him. Odysseus, from inside, heard his footsteps.

"I think some friend of yours is coming," Odysseus said to Eumaeus. "The dogs don't bark at him and I hear footsteps."

He had barely finished speaking when Telemachus appeared in the doorway. In amazement, Eumaeus jumped up, dropping the pot he'd been holding as he mixed the wine. He went up to his master and kissed his head and both his eyes and his hands. He greeted him the way a father greets his son who comes from a distant land, his only son whom he loves so much, for whom he has suffered greatly.

"Telemachus, you've returned!" he sobbed. "Sweet light of my eyes! I thought I'd never see you again."

"I'll do as you say, my good man. I've come here for your sake. I wanted to see you and to hear if my mother is still in the house or whether somebody has married her."

"Yes, truly, she stays with determined heart, but her nights are spent weeping in sorrow."

Eumaeus took Telemachus' spear as he stepped over the stone threshold. As Telemachus drew near Odysseus, his father got up to give him a place, but Telemachus stopped him. "Stay there, stranger, and we will find a seat somewhere else," Telemachus said.

Odysseus sat back down and Eumaeus put brushwood on the ground and a flecce on top of it. Telemachus sat on that next to his father. Then Eumaeus set before them platters of meat left over from the day before and heaped up bread in baskets and mixed wine in an ivy-wood bowl.

"Where did this stranger come from?" Telemachus asked Eumaeus when they had finished eating.

"Well, I'll tell you," Eumaeus answered. "He says he comes from Crete and that he's wandered through many men's cities. But now he's run away from a Thesprotian ship and come here. I'll put him in your hands. He says he is your suppliant."

"Eumaeus, what you say brings me pain. How can I welcome a stranger to my house? I'm still young and I don't think I could defend myself against the suitors. Let me offer him a cloak and a tunic and I will give him a sword and sandals and send him wherever he wants to go. Or if you prefer, you can keep him here at the farm. But I won't let him come among the arrogant nobles full of insolence! I'm afraid they will mock him and bring me grief."

"My friend," Odysseus interrupted, "you have disturbed me greatly. I wish I were as young as I once was, or that I were a son of Odysseus, or Odysseus himself, so that I could be a curse to those who defile his halls!"

"Well, stranger, I'll explain the situation to you," Telemachus answered. "As Laertes begot Odysseus, so did Odysseus father just one son: me. I have not brothers or cousins to support me. This is why a huge number of enemies are now in possession of my property – princes from nearby islands and those who live here in Ithaca, too. They court my mother and ravage my house. She can neither say 'No' to an ugly marriage, nor put a stop to their courting. They feast endlessly, and before long they will bring me to ruin. All this is in the lap of the gods, I suppose.

"But Eumaeus, go quickly up to the house and tell Penelope that I am safe, that I've returned from Pylos. But don't let any of the suitors find out, because some of them wish to harm me."

"I understand," Eumaeus said. "But come, tell me: should I find Laertes too? They say he hasn't eaten or drunk anything since the day you went to Pylos."

Telemachus said, "No. Give Penelope your message and then come back. Tell my mother to send Eurycleia, her maid, to inform the old man in secret."

Eumaeus took up his sandals and bound them under his feet and went up to the city.

Athena saw that Eumaeus had left the farm and she approached the hut in the likeness of a tall, beautiful woman, a skilled loom worker. She stood in the doorway and showed herself to Odysseus. Telemachus did not see her; the dogs did, but they did not bark. Instead, whining, they crept in fear to the furthest part of the farmyard.

Athena signalled to Odysseus with her brows, and he understood. He went out of the hut.

"Son of Laertes, tell your son your secret and don't hide who you are. Once the two of you have planned death for the suitors you can go to the city. I won't be long away from you. I am eager for the fight."

Athena touched him with her wand. She put a cloak and tunic about him and increased his stature and made him young again. His skin gained colour and his cheeks filled out and a dark beard grew on his chin. When she had transformed him, she left.

Odysseus went back inside the hut. His son was amazed when he saw him and terrified. He turned his eyes aside, thinking this was a god.

"Stranger, you don't seem to me as you just were! You are a god, one of those who holds heaven! Let us kill an animal in your honour and give you gifts of gold and then you can spare us! Be kind!"

"I am no god. I am your father, for whose sake you have suffered much." A tear fell from Odysseus' eye, although he tried to hold it back.

"You cannot be Odysseus, my father! Some god is tricking me so that

I may feel yet more pain. There's no way a mortal could do this. Just now you were an old man and wearing ragged clothes – now you're like the gods who live in the sky."

"Telemachus, be sure that I am Odysseus! I am here just as you see me, in my native land. It's Athena who makes me look however she wants. Now a beggar, now young, now wearing fine clothes. It's easy for gods both to glorify men and bring them down."

Then Odysseus sat and Telemachus threw his arms about him and they wailed shrill sounds, their cries like those of sea eagles with crooked talons whose chicks men have taken before they were fledged. This is how tears fell piteously from their eyes.

When the sun was setting, Telemachus suddenly asked, "How did you get here, dear father? Which sailors brought you here? Who were they?"

"Phaeacians brought me, men famous for their ships. They carried me asleep and set me down in Ithaca with gifts of bronze and gold and woven cloth. I've stowed these treasures in a cave. I've come to this hut at Athena's bidding, so we can plan how to destroy our enemies. Come now, how many nobles are there? Who are they?"

"Father, you can be sure that I know about your greatness as a spearman and your ability in counsel. But this would be too much. There are fifty-two from Dulichium and six slaves. From Cephalonia there are twenty-four. From Zacynthus there are twenty, and from Ithaca itself there are twelve. If we're going to meet all these men in the halls I'm afraid we'll have a hard time."

"Athena and Zeus are going to help us. Is that enough? Or do I still need other assistance?"

"Those are good allies, sitting in the clouds! They rule all humankind and the other gods too!"

"I don't think it will take long for those two gods to come to our assistance when the fighting starts," Odysseus said. "For now, go up to the house and join the insolent suitors. Later on, Eumaeus will take me into the city looking like a wretched beggar. And if they treat me badly, be calm, even if they drag me by the feet through the door and hurl things at me. Endure it. Tell them to stop and try to dissuade them with polite words that they'll pay no attention to.

"When Athena gives the signal, I'll nod to you. Take the weapons lying about in the hall and hide them away in the upstairs storeroom. When the nobles notice their arms are missing and ask about them, trick them and say, 'I've taken them out of the smoke because they are all grimy. And also I'm afraid that when you get heated with a little wine you may start quarrelling and somebody might get stabbed and bring shame on the feast!'

"But leave behind two swords for us, and two spears and two shields. As for the suitors, Athena and Zeus will bewitch them. Let nobody find out that Odysseus has come back. Don't let Laertes know, nor Eumaeus, nor anybody of the house, not even Penelope."

So they hatched their plans together. In the meantime, the ship that brought Telemachus and his men from Pylos sailed into the harbour below the city. They drew the ship up on shore. Men went to help them with the tackle and carry the gifts Telemachus had acquired, taking them to a secret house in the city.

They despatched a messenger to inform Penelope that Telemachus was back in the country. The messenger and Eumaeus met as they went up to the house. When they arrived, the messenger spoke out loud, standing in the middle of the female slaves:

"At this very moment, my queen, your son, whom you love so much, has come back!"

Eumaeus moved closer to Penelope and told her everything that her son had asked him to, then went on his way, back to his swine.

The nobles were much depressed when they heard this news.

"My friends, Telemachus has done a brazen deed," said Eurymachus. "We thought he would never pull it off. We need to gather together rowers, launch a ship and send word to those waiting for Telemachus in the channel to come back."

The words had barely left his mouth when Amphinomus looked down the hill and saw a ship in the deep harbour.

"I don't think we need to send a message," Amphinomus said, breaking into a jolly laugh, "for here are the men returned home. Some god must have told them what was going on. Maybe our friends saw Telemachus' ship but could not capture it."

They got up and went down to the shore, where the men were still busy with the tackle. Then the suitors went together to the town square, where Antinoüs stood in front of them all.

"Incredible! The gods have saved that man!" he said. "Every day our comrades sat on the heights, watch after watch, and when the sun went down we never spent a night on shore but kept sailing in our ship,

waiting for dawn, waiting for Telemachus, so we could capture and kill him. Meanwhile, some god has brought him home. But we'll find a way to destroy him. He won't escape. So long as he lives he thwarts our plans. He's a smart fellow and the people are not on our side.

"Come, before he calls the Ithacans to an assembly. He'll be seething with rage and he'll tell them how we plotted against him. The Ithacans won't like it when they hear this. They'll drive us out of here. Let's act now and kill him in a field far from the city. We'll take his property and divide it between us. His mother and whoever marries her can have the house . . .

"If you don't like this plan, and you want him to go on living and keep hold of his father's wealth, then let every man woo Penelope with gifts and seek to win her that way."

There was a deadly hush. Then Amphinomus spoke to the crowd. He was the leader of the nobles from Dulichium and the suitor who most pleased Penelope, thanks to his kind words and thoughtful manner. With good intent, he addressed the others:

"My friends, I don't think we should kill him, because it is a terrible thing to murder a member of the royal household. No, let us wait to see what the gods want. If Zeus approves, I'll kill him myself and encourage others to join me in this act, but if the gods are against us, let us desist."

They approved of what he said, and went back to Odysseus' house.

Penelope decided now to show herself to the insolent nobles, for she had learned of the threat to kill her son. She went down to the hall with her handmaids. She stood by the doorpost and held a shining veil before her face.

"Antinoüs, you violent man, you doer of evil!" she said. "You are supposed to be the best of your class. But you scheme death for my

Telemachus and have no care for suppliants protected by Zeus! It is evil to plot evil. Don't you know about the time when your father came to this house in fear of the mob? The people were angry because he had joined the Taphian pirates and harassed the Thesprotians who were allied with us. They wanted to kill him and take his property, which was vast. But Odysseus restrained them. It's his house that you now devour, and you court his wife and desire to kill his son. So please, stop! And I urge you to tell the others to stop!"

"Oh daughter of Icarius, wise Penelope," Eurymachus answered, "be happy! For as long as I see the light of the sun, any man who lays his hands on your son Telemachus will not keep his life. That man's black blood will flow around my spear! For Odysseus used to dandle me on his knee and put tastes of meat in my hands and let me try sips of red wine. So his son Telemachus is the dearest of all men to me, and I say he should have no fear of death, at least from men. As for the gods, this is out of our control."

Eurymachus' words were soothing, but in reality he was scheming death for her son. Penelope went back to her upper chamber and wept for Odysseus, her husband, until she fell asleep.

When evening came, Eumaeus returned to Odysseus and Telemachus in the hut. Athena came close to Odysseus and made him into an old man. She put wretched clothing on him so there was no risk of Eumaeus recognizing him and letting slip who he was to Penelope or someone else.

"You're back!' Telemachus said to Eumaeus. "What's the news? Have the proud nobles abandoned their ambush, or do they still lie in wait for me?"

Eumaeus answered, "I wanted to come back as soon as I'd given my message. But as I was leaving the city I saw a ship putting into the harbour. It was packed with men carrying shields and spears. I thought it was the suitors' ship but I'm not sure."

Telemachus smiled as he glanced at his father but avoided Eumaeus' eye. When they finished their meal they felt good and went to sleep.

Book 17

BEGGAR IN HIS OWN HOUSE

At dawn, Telemachus put on his sandals and took up his spear. He spoke to the swineherd.

"Eumaeus, good fellow, I'm going to visit my mother. Take this stranger to the city so that he can beg for food. I can't take care of it because I have so much else on my mind. If this makes the stranger angry, too bad for him."

"Go, my friend," Odysseus cut in. "That's fine. A beggar will have more luck in town than in the fields. I'm not young enough to stay on the farm and work. Go on, I'll make my way as soon as the sun is warmer. These clothes are wretched and there's a risk the morning frost would do me in, for you say the city is a long way away."

Telemachus walked rapidly through the farm, planning a deadly end for the suitors. When he reached his home, he leaned his spear against a pillar and crossed the stone threshold.

Eurycleia was first to see him. Breaking into sobs, she ran and embraced him, and all the other maids gathered around, kissing his head and shoulders in welcome.

Down came Penelope from her chamber, looking like Artemis or golden Aphrodite. She burst into tears and flung her arms about her son.

"You're back," she sobbed, "sweet light of my eyes. I thought I would never see you again. Come, tell me if you have news of your father."

"Mother, don't stir up my emotions again when I have only just managed to escape destruction. No, take a bath, put on fresh clothes, then

go to your room with your maids and tell the gods that you will sacrifice many animals in their honour if only Zeus will bring a day of reckoning to these evil men. I need to go to the town square so that I can invite to our house a stranger who travelled with me from Pylos. I told Peiraeus to take him home and look after him until I could come for him."

Penelope went to her bath, dressed in clean clothes and vowed to the gods that she would sacrifice many animals if only Zeus would wreak vengeance on the insolent suitors.

Grasping his spear, Telemachus strode into the hall with his two fine dogs. Athena showered grace over him and everybody stared when they saw him. The proud nobles gathered around him and spoke in respectful terms, but in their brooding hearts they planned wickedness. He avoided most of these men and sat down with Mentor and Halitherses, old friends of his father. Then Peiraeus appeared at the door, bringing with him the stranger Theoclymenus.

"Telemachus," said Peiraeus, "send some women to my house so I can deliver to you the treasures that Menelaüs presented you with."

"Peiraeus, it's not yet clear how things are going to play out. If these insolent nobles murder me in the hall and divide up my property, I want you to keep the gifts. But if I can bring about their deaths, I shall be glad to have you bring the treasure here to my house."

Telemachus led Peiraeus and Theoclymenus inside. They laid their cloaks on chairs and went into the bathing area. When the maids had washed them and rubbed their flesh with oil, they dressed them in cloaks and tunics. The two men came out into the main hall and sat down on chairs. A maid brought water and drew up tables beside them. The housekeeper set out bread and meat.

Penelope sat near Telemachus, spinning threads of yarn. She spoke so that only those close by could hear.

"I think I'll go upstairs and lie down on my bed of sorrow, wet with tears since Odysseus went to Troy. But you haven't yet told me whether you have heard anything about your father or his return."

"I'll tell you now, Mother. Nestor received me with great warmth, the way a father greets a son who has been gone a long time. He had heard nothing of Odysseus, whether he is alive or dead. He sent me on to Menelaüs. There I met Helen for whose sake the Trojans fought bitterly.

"Menelaüs asked me why I'd come to Sparta looking for my father, and he said, 'May those who court your mother go to the House of Hades! When a doe sets down her newborn fawns in the lion's den and disappears over the mountains and the grassy valleys seeking pasture, the lion who comes back to his den delivers the fawns a quick end. This is how Odysseus, like a lion, will bring doom to these men!'

"Menelaüs said he'd seen Odysseus on an island, in torment in the halls of Calypso who keeps him against his will. He cannot come back to his native land, for he has no ship or men to help him cross the sea. When I had established these facts, I set out for home. The gods sent a fair wind and brought me swiftly here."

Telemachus' words stirred her heart. Then Theoclymenus spoke up.

"Most honoured wife of Odysseus – Menelaüs does not see things clearly. Zeus be my witness, Odysseus is even now somewhere in his native land, learning of these wicked deeds and machinating against the suitors. I saw a bird of omen as I sat on the ship, and I informed Telemachus."

"Oh stranger, would that this might be the case!" Penelope answered. "Then you would receive my friendship and many gifts."

Meanwhile, outside in the courtyard, the suitors were playing games, the discus and the javelin, as was their insolent custom. When it was time for dinner, one of Odysseus' slaves summoned them in. A noble said: "Well men, let's go and prepare a feast!"

They went inside and set to killing sheep, fat goats, pigs and a heifer for a banquet.

Eumaeus and Odysseus were getting ready to walk from the countryside into the city.

"Stranger," said Eumaeus, "if you're so eager to reach the city today, then let's set off right away. The day is largely spent and you will get cold tonight."

Odysseus answered, "Let's go. But give me a staff if you have one someplace, for you said it was a rugged path."

Odysseus threw his threadbare pouch around his shoulders and Eumaeus gave him a staff. They set out. The other slaves stayed behind to guard the farm with the dogs. The swineherd led the way and Odysseus followed looking like a sad old beggar.

When they were close to the city they came to a fountain that supplied the townspeople with water. Above it sat an altar to the Nymphs, where passersby made offerings. Melanthius was there, driving his goats – he was bringing the best in his herds to the suitors to feast on. Melanthius insulted Eumaeus and the disguised Odysseus in the foulest way.

"Here now comes scum leading scum! As ever, the god brings like to like. Where are you leading this pest of a beggar who ruins our fine dining? He's a man who likes to beg for scraps, not for swords or tripods like a real man. He knows only trouble; he doesn't care to busy himself with work. He would rather go skulking around begging, feeding his bottomless belly. But I'll tell you this for nothing: if he comes to the palace of Odysseus, he'll find plenty of stools get hurled at his head!"

On his way past, he kicked Odysseus in the buttocks – but he did not dislodge Odysseus from the path. Odysseus considered killing Melanthius with his staff, or perhaps picking him up by the ears and smashing his head on the ground. He contained himself, however. Eumaeus looked Melanthius in the eye and rebuked him, lifting his hands in prayer:

"Nymphs, daughters of Zeus, if ever Odysseus burned thigh pieces on your altar, grant that my master comes back, and that he scatters the airs that this goatherd puts on while roaming around the city, a bad herdsman ruining his flocks."

"Ah, look how this dog talks! He's nothing but trouble. I hope that Apollo strikes down Telemachus, or that the nobles might just kill him, finishing him off the same way Odysseus has died in some distant land."

Melanthius hurried on and arrived at the palace. He went inside and sat down among the nobles. The maids brought in meat and bread. Outside, approaching with Eumaeus, Odysseus heard the sound of the lyre, for Phemius was striking a few chords ready to sing.

"Eumaeus, surely this is the beautiful house of Odysseus," Odysseus said, clasping the swineherd by the hand. "It's obvious straightaway. There's building after building, and the court is built with strong walls and the double gates are well constructed. Nobody could breach them. It seems as though men are feasting inside – I smell meat and hear the sounds of the lyre."

"Well, you see now what goes on," said Eumaeus. "But come, let us think. Either you enter first while I remain here, or if you prefer, I'll go first and you follow. But don't linger outside for long, or someone may see you and throw something or hit you!"

"I hear what you say. You go in and I'll wait here. I'm not unused to blows. I've been through a lot on the sea and in war. Let this be added to what's already happened."

A dog lying there raised his head and pricked up his ears – Argus, Odysseus' dog whom he bred in the old days. In the past, young men used to take Argus out to hunt wild goats and deer and rabbits, but now he was neglected, his master gone. He lay in a pile of mule and cattle dung, one of many heaped around waiting to be taken away by Odysseus' slaves as fertilizer for his lands. When Argus sensed that Odysseus was near he wagged his tail and dropped his ears. But he did not have the strength to come closer to his master. Odysseus looked in the other direction and wiped away a tear.

"Eumaeus, it's odd that this dog lies here in the dung. He's a good-looking animal."

"Yes, this is the dog of a king. If he were on form, the way he was when Odysseus left for Troy, you'd be amazed by his speed and power. No animal could outrun him, and he was the best at tracking. But now evil times have fallen on him, and his master has perished and the women give him no care."

So saying, Eumaeus went into the house to join the suitors. As for Argus, now that he had seen Odysseus, black death seized him.

When Eumaeus entered the hall, Telemachus was first to notice him, and he nodded and summoned him to his side. Eumaeus took the stool normally used by the carver and put it next to Telemachus' table and sat down. A slave set meat and bread before him.

Not long behind him came Odysseus, looking like a beggar. Telemachus called Eumaeus to him. He took a whole loaf from the basket and filled it with all the meat it could hold.

"Eumaeus, take this and give it to the stranger and then tell him to beg from the nobles."

Eumaeus went over and said to Odysseus: "Stranger, Telemachus gives you these and suggests you beg of the nobles."

"King Zeus, I pray that Telemachus may be blessed among men and be granted everything he desires!" Odysseus replied.

Odysseus took the food and put it in his pouch. He ate while the minstrel was entertaining everyone. When Phemius stopped singing, the nobles broke into shouts of merriment. Athena drew near Odysseus and told him to go among the suitors and gather bits of bread and discover which men were decent and which were lawless. Either way, she didn't intend to save even a single one of them from death.

He began on the right, stretching out his hand as though he were accustomed to begging. They took pity on him and gave him food, staring at him curiously and asking who he was and where he came from.

"Hear me, you who want to marry the glorious queen," Melanthius the goatherd said. "I have seen this stranger before! The swineherd brought him here, but I have no idea where he appeared from."

"Why did you bring this man to the city?" Antinoüs rebuked Eumaeus. "Don't we have enough drifters?"

"Antinoüs, these are not kind words," Eumaeus said, "although you are of good birth. You are harsh to Odysseus' slaves, and to me most of all."

"Don't talk, Eumaeus," said Telemachus. "Don't waste words on this man. Antinoüs always does this; he likes to provoke anger by speaking cruelly and encouraging others to do the same."

Then he addressed Antinoüs directly.

"So, Antinoüs, you prefer to eat my food yourself rather than give something to another!"

"What a delightful thing to say!" Antinoüs answered. "Very spirited!" He picked up the footstool that he usually rested his feet on while he dined.

The other suitors were doling out scraps, filling the beggar's pouch with bread and meat. Odysseus was on his way back to the threshold to leave when he stopped next to Antinoüs.

"My friend, give me a gift," he said. "You don't seem to be the worst of men. You look like a king. It is fitting that you give me a bigger hunk of bread than the rest.

"You know, I too once dwelt in a large house. I was rich and I often gave to vagabonds. I had more slaves than I could count and all the other luxuries that mean men live well. But Zeus reduced me to nothing. He dispatched me with pirates to Egypt. I sent out scouts, but my men were arrogant and immediately set about laying waste to the fields. They carried off the women and children and killed the men. A cry went up that reached the city, and at daybreak the people spilled onto the plain, filling it with warriors and chariots and flashing bronze. Zeus spread panic over my men and we were surrounded by the enemy. Many were killed, and the others were led to the city to be slaves. They handed me over to someone they knew who took me to Cyprus, to a man named Dmetor, the ruler there. And from Cyprus I have come here, in much distress."

"What god has brought this nasty thing here to ruin our feasting?" Antinoüs said. "Get away from me! You are a shameless beggar!"

"Can this be true?" said Odysseus drawing back. "You would not give a grain of salt from your own stores to a suppliant, you who sit at another man's table? Couldn't you take a morsel of bread and give it away? You have plenty."

Antinoüs became still more angry. "I don't think that you will get out of this hall in one piece," he said with a glance from beneath his brow, "now that you've stooped to insults." He threw the footstool and it hit Odysseus on the shoulder – but he stood firm as a rock. He shook his head, contemplating evil, then went back over to the threshold and sat down.

"Hear me, you noble suitors of the glorious queen," he said aloud. "I wish to say something. If beggars have gods and Furies, may the doom of death come on Antinoüs before his wedding day!"

"Sit still and eat, stranger," Antinoüs answered, "or go elsewhere, or men will drag you by your hands and feet through the house for words like these and strip off all your skin!"

But the nobles were indignant and started saying: "Antinoüs, you should not have struck this unfortunate wanderer. Are you doomed? What if an immortal comes from heaven? The gods do this; they appear disguised as strangers from distant lands, and they put on different shapes and visit the cities."

Antinoüs paid no attention. Telemachus was angry that his father had been struck, but he let no tears fall. He shook his head in silence, planning revenge.

Wise Penelope, sitting in her chamber upstairs, heard about the man being struck in the hall.

"May Apollo the Archer cut them down!" she said to her handmaids.

"Grant that our prayers be answered!" one of them replied. "Then not one of these men will be alive tomorrow morning."

"I hate them," said Penelope. "They are evil. But Antinoüs is the worst of all. He is like death. A stranger goes through the house asking for a little something and all the others fill his pouch, but Antinoüs throws a footstool and hits him on the shoulder!"

Meanwhile, downstairs, Odysseus was eating his dinner. Penelope went out of her chamber to the stairway and called to Eumaeus.

"Go, Eumaeus, ask the stranger to come here," she said when he appeared. "I want to greet him and ask if maybe he's heard anything about Odysseus or has seen him, even."

Eumaeus replied, "I hosted him for three nights and days. He told me the story of his sufferings. He says he has an ancestral connection with Odysseus. He lives in Crete. And he says that he has heard of Odysseus, that he's nearby in the land of the Thesprotians and he's bringing riches."

"Go call him so that he can tell me this face to face. As for all these men, let them carry on. Their own possessions lie untouched in their own halls. But they pile into our house day after day, killing our cattle and sheep and goats, drinking and making merry. The wine flows recklessly, they create chaos abusing our valuable property, and there's no man to stave off ruin. But if Odysseus ever came back, he and his son would take vengeance."

As she spoke, Telemachus sneezed loudly and the whole room echoed. Penelope laughed.

"Go, I beg you, call the stranger here before me! See how my son sneezed at my words? This means certain death will fall on these men, one and all, and not a single person will escape."

Eumaeus went down to the hall and approached Odysseus.

"My good man, stranger, you are called for by Penelope, the mother of Telemachus. She wants to ask you about her husband."

"Eumaeus, I will tell the truth to wise Penelope. But I'm afraid of this throng of suitors. A moment ago when I was going through the hall this man struck me, and neither Telemachus nor anybody else lifted a finger. Ask Penelope to wait till the sun sets and then she can question me about her husband as we sit by the fire."

The swineherd went back to Penelope's chamber and told her.

"You didn't bring him, Eumaeus? What does he mean by this? A bashful beggar is a poor one!"

"I think he's right to be wary of the insolence of the men. He wants you to wait till the sun sets. Anyway, it's better for you to speak to him alone."

"I agree. There's no one in the world as wicked as these men."

So she spoke, and Eumaeus went back down to the crowd of suitors. He went up to Telemachus and held his head close so the others could not hear.

"Master, I'm leaving now to take care of the pigs and see to the farm.

Keep safe. Be careful, for these nobles are plotting evil. May Zeus destroy them before harm falls on us!"

"Fine, my good friend. Go, but first have some dinner. And in the morning come back. I'll take care of the situation here, with the help of the gods."

The swineherd sat down on a polished chair. When he had finished eating he left the hall full of banqueters. Those men made merry with dance and song, for it was evening.

Book 18

THE BEGGAR'S CHALLENGE

In the town of Ithaca there lived a beggar with a ravenous belly. He had no strength, no power, but he was a hulking great man. Arnaeus was the name his mother gave him, but everybody called him Irus because he ran errands like Iris, the messenger goddess. He wished to drive Odysseus out of his own house.

"Get away, old man, or you will be dragged out! Get lost, or a quarrel may come to blows!"

"You fool, I do you no harm," Odysseus replied, with an angry glance. "This threshold is big enough for the two of us. We beggars depend on the gods for our prosperity. But be careful about challenging me. Although I'm old I will bloody your chest and lips, and you won't be back for more."

"Look how this filthy pig talks!" the tramp said. "Like an old kitchen maid! I'll fix him, scattering all his teeth on the ground."

Antinoüs heard them and broke into a laugh.

"My friends, a god has sent sport to this house."

The suitors sprang up, entertained, and gathered around.

"Listen, my friends," Antinoüs said. "There are goats' stomachs lying around the fire, stuffed with fat and blood. Whichever of you two wins, let him choose any stomach he wants."

"There is no way an old man, overcome with suffering, can fight with a younger man," Odysseus said. "Nonetheless, my belly pushes me on. All right, we can fight, but all of you swear an oath that none of you will hit me."

The suitors swore not to strike him.

"Stranger," said Telemachus, breaking in, "don't be afraid of these men. If any of them attack you, he will have to fight me as well."

Odysseus tucked up his rags, revealing his broad shoulders and his powerful arms. Athena came close and made his limbs even mightier. The nobles were astonished, and muttered:

"I think that Irus will be in big trouble against this grandpa!"

Irus was shaken too and trembled.

"My little braggart, don't tremble before this fellow," Antinoüs upbraided him. "He is old and overcome by suffering. If he beats you, I will throw you into a ship and send you to the mainland to King Echetus who will cut off your nose and ears and rip out your balls and give them raw to dogs!"

Irus trembled even more. They led him into the ring and both men put up their hands. Odysseus couldn't decide whether he should kill him or strike him a light blow and stretch him on the ground – but the second course seemed better, so the suitors wouldn't realize who he was. Irus hit him on the shoulder, but Odysseus struck him on the neck beneath the ear and crushed the bones, so that dark red ran from his mouth as he fell down in the dust and gnashed his teeth and kicked the ground. The nobles raised their hands and laughed loudly.

Odysseus seized Irus by the foot and dragged him into the courtyard where he propped him against the wall. He placed his staff in his hand.

"Sit there now, and scare off the pigs and dogs. Stop lording it over strangers and beggars, you fool, or you may win an even greater disaster."

Odysseus went back into the hall. He sat down on the threshold. Antinoüs set before him a stomach filled with fat and blood, and Amphinomus took two loaves of bread from the basket and placed them alongside. Then Amphinomus held out a cup of gold filled with wine.

"Hail to you, stranger! May good fortune be yours in times to come, you who now are beset by sorrows," he said.

"You seem to be a man of some wisdom," Odysseus answered. "Your

father was a wise man too. I've heard that he was brave and wealthy, Nisus of Dulichium. So I will tell you. Nothing is more feeble than man, of all creatures that breathe. He thinks he will never suffer as long as the gods are on his side, but when the gods bring misfortune, he must endure his sorrow with as much patience as he can.

"So let no man be lawless but endure whatever the gods send him without complaint. Look at the wantonness which you men display, dishonouring the wife of a man who will soon be back in his native land. He is near. Go to your homes so that you do not meet him. There will be no departure without bloodshed when he comes home!"

Odysseus poured an offering of wine from the golden cup, drank and gave back the cup to Amphinomus, who bowed his head, much depressed.

In her chambers, Penelope spoke to Eurynomê.

"Eurynomê, I want to let the nobles see me now, even though this is unprecedented and I hate them. Also, I want to say something to my son, to make him stop consorting with these haughty men who speak to him respectfully but really mean him harm."

"This makes good sense, my child. Go, say what you want to your son once you have washed yourself and oiled your face. Do not present yourself with tear-stained cheeks."

"Eurynomê, I know you love me, but the gods destroyed the beauty that once was mine the day Odysseus left in his ships. Ask two of my women to come to me, so that I do not go alone into a room full of men."

Eurynomê went out to fetch two women. As she did so, Athena shed sleep over Penelope. While she slumbered, she gave her gifts. She cleansed Penelope's face with the oil that Aphrodite uses when she goes to the dances of the Graces. Athena made her taller and more stately and whiter than freshly sawn ivory.

The goddess departed and the maids arrived. Sleep left Penelope. She rubbed her cheeks.

"Ah, sweet sleep took me . . . I wish that Artemis would come to me at this very moment and give me a sweet death, so that I finally stop wasting away longing for my husband . . ."

She got up and went to stand by the pillar by the doorway of the main hall, her face hidden beneath a veil. On either side of her stood a faithful maid. Instantly, the suitors were enchanted by her and consumed with lust.

"Telemachus, you're not as clear-thinking as you once were," she said. "Even when you were little you acted with more intelligence. Now that you are grown, with all the appearance of a rich man's son, you don't seem so upright. What if the stranger in our house should come to some harm? The shame of it would fall on you."

"Mother, I don't blame you for being angry. I am aware of what's going on, the good and the bad. But it's hard for me to think straight when I'm surrounded by these men making their evil plans and I have no one to help me!"

"Daughter of Icarius, Penelope," interrupted Eurymachus, "if all the Achaeans could see you, still more would be feasting in your halls. You surpass all women with your beauty and good sense."

"Eurymachus, the gods ruined my beauty when the Achaeans departed for Troy, taking Odysseus with them. If he would only come back and take care of me, then I'd be far more famous and beautiful. But as it is I'm weighed down with sorrow, I've suffered so much.

"But when he went away, didn't he say this? 'My wife, not all the Achaeans will return, for the Trojans are men of war, hurlers of the spear, drawers of the bow, drivers of horses. I don't know whether a god will bring me back or whether I'll be cut down in the land of Troy. You must take care of everything here – my father and mother especially. And when you see my son growing a beard, that is the time to choose whom to marry and leave your house.'

"Those were his words, and now his predictions are coming true. The night is near when a hateful marriage must be my lot. Zeus has stolen my

happiness. It grieves me too the manner in which you men present your suit – this has never been the way it is done. If you wish to marry a lady of worth, and if you are competing with one another, you should bring cattle and sheep and host a banquet and shower her with dazzling gifts. Do not devour the livelihood of another without paying!"

Odysseus was happy because Penelope was tricking the suitors.

"Daughter of Icarius, wise Penelope, let any Achaean who wishes to offer gifts do so, and it's right that you accept them," Antinoüs said. "It's not prudent to refuse a gift. But we will not go back to our lands or anywhere else until you choose one of us to marry!"

So each man sent a slave to bring gifts. Antinoüs' men brought in a beautiful embroidered robe with golden brooches that had a clever tubular clasp. Eurymachus' slaves offered a gold chain strung with amber beads, bright like the sun. Amphinomus presented drop earrings, each with three jewelled clusters as big as mulberries. Another man proffered a necklace of surpassing beauty. Gift upon gift was brought in. Then Penelope went to her upper chamber, her handmaids walking behind her bearing the presents.

The suitors turned to dancing, song and merry-making. Night came and they set up three braziers in the hall. Handmaids lit the torches.

"Slaves of Odysseus," Odysseus said to the maids, "go upstairs and spin yarn by Penelope's side. Cheer her up. I will keep these torches alight. If the men want to stay up all night, I can manage."

The slaves burst out laughing. Melantho scolded Odysseus. Even though Penelope had raised Melantho like a daughter, Melantho was not sympathetic to her as she was in love with Eurymachus.

"You wretch, you must be crazy! Why don't you go and beg elsewhere? You keep talking, on and on, in the company of men who matter. You feel no fear at all! I think the wine's made you take leave of your senses. Or are you so full of yourself because you beat up Irus? Just be careful that a better man doesn't jump up and smack you around the head and make your blood gush out as he chases you from the house!"

Odysseus was very angry.

"I'll tell Telemachus what you say," he replied, "so that he cuts you limb from limb."

The women ran away in terror because they believed he meant it. Odysseus took his stand by the burning braziers. He looked at the nobles. He was thinking terrible thoughts, which would soon become reality.

But Athena prompted the suitors to be even more outrageous, to make Odysseus angrier still.

"Hear me, all you who hope to marry this resplendent queen," said Eurymachus. "It's the gods that have sent this man to Odysseus' house. Look, the torches reflecting off his bald head make him gleam!"

He called out to Odysseus.

"Stranger, maybe you'd like to work for me? I could take you in on an outlying farm. You can gather stones for my walls and plant trees. I'll give you plenty of food, clothe you and give you sandals. But, of course, since you have learned only wicked ways in life, you won't want to bother yourself with real work. Carry on on skulking around instead so you can feed your insatiable belly!"

"Eurymachus, I only wish we could have a contest on a long summer's day," Odysseus answered. "We can each have a scythe and work on the tall grass, fasting till late evening. Oh, or I wish there were oxen to drive, the best ones, well fed, of the same age, strong enough to carry the yoke, tireless. And let's say there's a field of four acres. Then you would see whether I could cut a straight furrow to the end. Or, how about Zeus brings us war and I have a shield and two spears and a helmet of bronze . . . then you would see me in the foremost of fighters and you wouldn't be making these sorts of comments. But you are an insolent man, and cruel. I suppose you think you're great and mighty because you spend your time with just a few weak men. If Odysseus came back, you would soon discover that those doors are not wide enough for you to flee through."

Eurymachus was infuriated.

"You wretch! I will punish you soon because you talk like this, in the company of real men! I think you're so drunk you're babbling nonsense. Or are you full of yourself because you beat that fool Irus?"

He picked up a footstool and threw it just as Odysseus sat down at the knees of Amphinomus. The stool struck a cupbearer and the wine jug clanged on the ground. The nobles guffawed, and the men said to each other:

"I wish that this stranger had died somewhere in his wanderings before he ever reached here. Then he wouldn't have brought this trouble among us."

"You are mad, you men, to disrespect a guest!" said Telemachus. "And you can no longer hide your drunkenness. Some god must be playing you. But now that you have eaten and drunk a lot, go ahead and take a rest . . ."

At Telemachus' words they bit their lips, astonished that he had spoken so boldly.

"My friends, I don't think that anybody could be angry because somebody has spoken fairly," Amphinomus said. "So let's not abuse this stranger anymore, or anybody else. No, come, let's put a little wine in our cups, pour out offerings and go home to rest. As for the stranger, let's just leave him here. Telemachus can take care of him."

A bowl of wine was mixed by a slave, the wine served out, offerings poured, the wine drunk. Then each man went to his house to take his rest.

Book 19

THE SCAR REVEALED

Odysseus was left in the hall, planning how to kill the suitors. He spoke quickly to Telemachus.

"Telemachus, hide away the weapons of war, and when the suitors ask you about them, trick them by saying, 'I've taken them out of the smoke to be cleaned. Also, I'm afraid that you will get into a drunken quarrel and bring shame on our feast. For the iron draws men to a fight.'"

Telemachus agreed and he called to Eurycleia. "Nurse, come here. I want you to keep the women shut up in their rooms while I transport the magnificent weapons to the storeroom so that smoke from the fires will not tarnish them."

"Yes, my child," Eurycleia answered. "I like that you're always considering the palace and the valuables inside it! But who will carry a light for you?"

"This stranger here will do it. I won't allow anybody to be idle in my house."

She locked the doors of the hall. Telemachus and Odysseus carried away the helmets and shields and the spears of bronze. Athena, invisible, walked ahead of them bearing a golden lamp.

"Father, this is extraordinary!" said Telemachus. "I can see the walls of the house as if from the light of a blazing fire! There must be a god among us, one of the immortals who lives in heaven."

Odysseus replied, "Do not second-guess the ways of those who live on

Olympus. Go now and take your rest. I'll stay here. Your mother has many questions for me."

Telemachus went to his chamber, but he could not sleep all night. Odysseus was left behind in the hall, plotting the death of the suitors with Athena's aid.

Then Penelope emerged from her quarters, looking like Artemis or Aphrodite. The maids set up a chair inlaid with spirals of ivory for her, by the fireside. Penelope sat down and they began to take away the food, the tables and the wine cups that the men had been using. They threw embers onto the hearth and piled on new logs to radiate light and warmth.

"Stranger, are you going to plague us all night long?" asked Melantho, scolding Odysseus yet again. "Go outside, you repulsive man, or I'm going to hit you with a torch!"

"Why do you attack me so angrily?" replied Odysseus. "Is it because I beg? I do it because I have to. Once I was rich and lived in a wealthy house, and I often showed charity to wanderers. But Zeus has brought me to this place. So be careful – perhaps one day your mistress will become disgusted with you and grow angry, or Odysseus will come home. There's still hope. But even if Odysseus is dead, his son is here in his place. He's no longer a child."

"Don't think that your conduct is hidden from me!" Penelope rebuked Melantho. "You knew quite well that I wanted to talk to the stranger about my husband! Eurynomê, bring me a chair and lay a fleece on it so the stranger may sit down and tell his story."

Eurynomê brought a chair and set it down.

"Stranger, who are you among men? And from where do you come? Where is your city, and where are your parents?"

"My lady, no one could find fault with you whose fame rises high as the sky. So ask me about anything, but not about my lineage or my native land.

I'm afraid that you would only fill my heart with more pain. I am a man of many sorrows. But it's not right to sit weeping in someone else's house. I don't want one of your maids or you yourself to be angry and say that I swim in tears because I have drunk too much."

"Stranger," said his wife, "I'm afraid that the gods destroyed all my beauty the day the Achaeans went to Troy and my husband Odysseus with them. If he would only come back and take care of me, my fame and beauty would be greater. But now I lament the many pains that some god has brought me. The princes of the nearby islands and those who live here court me against my will and devastate my house!

"I came up with a deceitful scheme. I set up a large loom, very wide, for a cloth of fine thread, and I told the suitors, 'Young men, you must wait, though you're eager for my hand. I have to finish this weaving. It's a shroud for Laertes, ready for when death will overcome him.'

"They agreed to this. By day I would weave, but at night I unravelled the cloth. For three years I kept the suitors from realizing my deceit. But when the fourth year came, then my shameless maids caught me out. So I completed the shroud.

"And now I can't escape this marriage. My parents urge me to wed and my son is upset because these men burn through his wealth. He is a man now and able to care for a house honoured by Zeus.

"Anyway, tell me your lineage. From where do you come? I don't think you came out of an oak tree or a stone!"

"Revered wife of Odysseus, will you never stop asking me about my lineage? Well, I'll tell you. There is a land called Crete. It's a fair, rich land, surrounded by water. Many men live there, in ninety cities. They speak a variety of different tongues. Among their great cities is Cnossus, where Minos reigned. He was the father of my father, Deucalion, and Idomeneus was my older brother. Idomeneus set sail in his ships to Troy. My name is Aithon, 'Blazing'.

"I saw Odysseus and loaded him with gifts. The wind had brought him to Crete as he was making for Troy. He anchored his ships in a difficult harbour and barely escaped the storm. He went up to the city and asked for Idomeneus, for he said that he was his friend. But Idomeneus had departed for Troy. I took him home and entertained him. For twelve days North Wind penned them in – it blew so hard they could scarcely stand on their feet. But on the thirteenth day the wind dropped and they set out to sea."

And so Odysseus made the many lies of his story seem like the truth. As Penelope listened her tears flowed like snow melting on the high mountains, fast-flowing swollen streams. Her lovely cheeks were wet as she wept, mourning her husband who was sitting right beside her. Odysseus felt pity for his loving wife, but with cunning he hid his tears. When she had finished crying, she answered him.

"Now, stranger, I must test you to find out whether you really saw my husband. Describe to me what kind of clothing he was wearing and what sort of man he was, and tell me about the men who followed him."

"Lady, it was so long ago, but I'll share with you what I remember. He was wearing a purple cloak with a double fold and a brooch of gold with double clasps, and on the brooch was a hound that held a fawn. Everybody marvelled at the detailed craftmanship, how the hound, moulded from gold, gazed at the fawn as it strangled it and the fawn writhed with its feet as it tried to get away. I remember the tunic he wore, too: sheer, soft and glistening.

"I don't know whether these are the sort of clothes he wore at home or whether one of his men gave them to him when he got on board, or maybe even a stranger, because Odysseus was a friend to many and few could equal him. I gave him a bronze sword and a beautiful cloak with a double fold and a fringed tunic, and I sent him off with honour on his ship.

"He had a man with him, who was a little older. He was round-shouldered, with dark skin and curly hair. His name was Eurybates."

Penelope's urge to weep was more intense than ever because she recognized these tokens.

"Truly, stranger, I pitied you before – but now I shall honour you, for it was I who gave Odysseus the clothes you describe. I folded them and brought them out of the storeroom and I added the golden brooch . . . but I will never welcome him back to his native land. It was an evil fate that sent him away in a ship to the accursed land of Troy!"

"Revered wife of Odysseus, don't let your heart dissolve in weeping. Not that I blame you. Any woman would lament the loss of her husband, the man whose children she has borne, who she has lain with in love – whether or not he is as great a man as Odysseus. But stop crying, and I will tell you the truth.

"Recently, I heard of Odysseus' return, how he's near, in the rich land of the Thesprotians. He's still alive! He's bringing many treasures back with him. But he's lost his men and his ship on his journey home. They perished at sea, but Odysseus washed up on the shore of the Phaeacians. They honoured him and gave him gifts and were glad to send him home.

"At least, that's what the king of the Thesprotians told me, and he swore that the ship was ready to transport him to his native land. But he sent me on my way first, for a Thesprotian ship happened to be setting out for

Dulichium. He showed me the riches that Odysseus had gathered. There was so much wealth there that it would feed even the tenth generation of his children. But Odysseus, he said, had gone to visit Dodona, to consult an oracle from the high oaks of Zeus.

"So, I tell you he's safe and will soon be back. I'll give you my word, and Zeus be my witness, that these things will come to pass! In the course of this very month, Odysseus will return."

"Ah stranger, I wish that this story of yours could come true. Then I would reward you at once with every kindness and plentiful gifts. But this is how I see it: Odysseus will never come home.

"All the same, my maids will wash your feet and fix up a bed and give you a cloak and covers so you may sleep till dawn. And early in the morning they will bathe you and anoint you ready to breakfast. For who will think me good if strangers are left to eat in my halls unwashed and in poor clothing? Humans don't live long. The hard hearted bring trouble on themselves during their lifetime and are mocked after death. The blameless, however, those who have an innocent heart, have their fame spread far and wide by their guests, and their name praised."

"Revered wife of Odysseus, after all my wanderings, cloaks and pretty covers don't please me any more, and I would be ashamed for a woman to touch my feet, unless there is some faithful old servant who has suffered pains like me."

"Dear stranger, you are wise and cautious in your words. I do have an old woman with an understanding heart who tended to my unlucky husband. She could wash your feet.

"Come now, Eurycleia, get up and bathe the feet of a man who is the same age as your master. These feet look like the feet of Odysseus, and the hands are similar too."

Eurycleia hid her face in her palms and shed tears as she remembered her absent master.

"Oh, I'm sorry, my child, my darling Odysseus," she said, "that I can do so little for you. Zeus hated you above all men, you who respected the gods. I suppose people mock the stranger when he comes to a famous house, just as your maids, those brazen creatures, mock this man. It is to avoid insult from them that he won't let them wash his feet, but he wants me to, and I don't mind. I will wash his feet for Penelope's sake and for your own."

The old woman took up a cauldron and poured in cold water and added hot. Odysseus sat down at the hearth and turned towards the darkness, for he immediately worried that she might realize the truth.

She began to wash her master and straight away recognized the scar which long ago a boar had given him. It happened when Odysseus went to Parnassus to visit Autolycus, his mother's father – the best of all men at thievery. Autolycus had visited Ithaca when Odysseus was just a newborn babe. Eurycleia put the child on his knees and said, "Autolycus, find a name now to give to your grandchild."

"I'll give you a name," Autolycus replied. "Because I have come here as one that has caused pain to many, let the baby be called Odysseus, which means 'man of anger'. When he's fully grown he may come to the house of his mother's family at Parnassus and I will give him many presents."

That was the reason why Odysseus went to Parnassus. Autolycus and his sons greeted him. His grandmother, Amphithea, took Odysseus in her arms and kissed his head and his beautiful eyes. Autolycus called to his sons to prepare a meal, and they brought in a five-year-old bull, skinned him, cut up the limbs, then pierced the slices with spits that they roasted. All day long until sunset they feasted happily. When the sun set and darkness came on, they lay down to rest and fell asleep.

As soon as dawn appeared, the men went out to hunt with the dogs. They climbed up the steep mountain Parnassus. The dogs ran ahead, tracking a scent, and behind them Odysseus followed, shaking his spear. Nearby, a big wild boar lay in a shelter so thick the strong winds could never blow through it; nor could it be pierced by the sun's rays or the driving rain, and fallen leaves were everywhere. The noise of men and dogs surrounded the boar and he came out of his lair with bristling back, his eyes flashing fire. Odysseus rushed forwards first of all and raised his spear, eager to stab the animal, but the boar was too quick and, charging sideways, gouged him above the knee, opening a long gash in the flesh. Odysseus speared him in the right shoulder. Clear through went the spear, and the boar fell in the dust with a cry as his life left him.

The sons of Autolycus took care of the carcass and bound up Odysseus' wound, stemming the black blood with a charm. They went straight back to their father's house. When they had healed Odysseus and given him gifts, they sent him back to his native land. Then Odysseus' father, Laertes, and his mother, Anticlea, rejoiced in his return and asked how he got his wound. He told them how the boar had scarred him with its white tusk when he was out hunting at Parnassus with the sons of Autolycus.

When Eurycleia felt the scar, she remembered it and let his leg drop into the basin, tipping it over, and the clanging bronze rang through the hall. She felt both joy and terror, and her eyes filled with tears. She touched Odysseus' chin.

"You are Odysseus, surely, dear child, and I did not know you until I handled your body!"

She looked towards Penelope, who did not realize that her husband was at home. Penelope didn't meet her glance because her thoughts were elsewhere. Odysseus drew Eurycleia closer to him.

"Do you want to destroy me? You yourself nursed me at your own breast. After suffering many torments I've come, after twenty years, to my house. But be silent in case someone hears us."

"My child, how can you ask! You know I am totally dependable. I shall be as silent as stone or iron."

Eurycleia went to fetch more water because the cauldron had spilled. Once she had washed Odysseus and anointed him with oil, Odysseus drew his chair close to the fire to warm himself and hid the scar with his rags.

"Stranger, I must ask, before we take our rest," said Penelope. "Or take what rest we can, anyone who can sleep in spite of their cares. The daughter of Pandareus, the nightingale, sings sweetly in the spring as she sits in the leaves of the trees, pouring out her voice with many trilling notes – wailing for her beloved child Itylus, whom she killed with the sword herself, unawares. My heart is torn, like hers.

"But come now, hear this dream. I had twenty geese in my house and my heart burst with joy as I watched them. But then a huge eagle with crooked talons swooped down from the mountain. He broke their necks and killed them. They lay strewn in a heap in the halls while he flew back up to the skies. I wept – it was a dream, of course – and round about me thronged the Achaean women as I wailed because the eagle had killed my geese. Then the eagle came back again and perched on a roof beam and in the voice of a man said, 'Be happy, daughter of Icarius. This is no dream but a true vision of good to come. The geese are the nobles, and I, who was once an eagle, have come back as your husband to bring an ugly end to these men.'

"So he spoke, and I woke up. Looking around, I saw the geese in the halls, feeding on wheat from their trough in the usual fashion."

"My lady, I cannot interpret this dream any other way. You can be sure ·that Odysseus himself is showing you events to come. For the suitors, destruction is clear. Not one of them will escape."

"Stranger, I know that dreams are hazy and you can't tell what they really mean. Certainly, not all of them become reality. For there are two gates of dreams. One is made of ivory. The dreams that pass through the gate of ivory deceive us with their empty words. But those that come through the gate of horn come true. I don't believe my dream came from that gate, though both I and my son would welcome that it had.

"I'll tell you something else. I'm going to set up a contest. I will remove the handles from twelve axes and line up the axe heads in a neat row, in a ditch in the hall. The challenge will be for the suitors to string a bow and shoot an arrow through the lined-up holes of the axe heads. Then I'll leave with the man who shoots the bow successfully and say farewell to this beautiful house filled with rich things which I shall always remember in my dreams."

"Dear wife of Odysseus, do not delay this contest, for I tell you that Odysseus will be here before these men have even strung the bow and shot it through the iron."

"If you could only stay here and comfort me I would never fall asleep," said Penelope, "but it is not possible to stay awake for ever. I will retire, then, to my chamber and lay down on my bed, stained with tears since the day Odysseus went to that evil Troy. You lie here in the hall on the floor, or the maids can set up a bed for you."

So saying, she went to her upper chamber, with her handmaids. When she got there she bewailed Odysseus, her husband, until Athena cast sleep on her eyes.

Book 20

THEOCLYMENUS' PROPHECY

Odysseus lay down on the floor, on an ox hide and sheep fleeces from the animals killed by the suitors. Eurynomê threw a cloak over him. He lay sleepless, his mind churning as he contemplated how to deliver death to the nobles. There was the sound of merry laughter from the hall as women who had been having sex with the suitors took their leave. Like a bitch who stands over her pups growling when she sees an unfamiliar face, Odysseus' heart growled at the suitors' actions.

But he hit his breast, saying to himself, "Take it easy. You had it worse when the Cyclops devoured your men, and you coped until your quick wits found you a way to escape that cave where you thought you were going to die."

So he scolded his own heart. He tossed this way and that, wondering how he might get his hands on the suitors, just one man against so many.

Then Athena came to him in the form of a woman.

"Why are you still awake, most unfortunate of men? This is your house and your wife is here, and your child, a fine man of whom anyone would be proud."

"Yes, goddess, but I'm trying to fathom how I can lay my hands on the nobles, single-handed against their gang. And I'm wondering how – even if I do kill them, with Zeus' help and yours – I will manage to escape vengeance from their relatives."

"You stubborn man! Other people place their trust in mere mortals far weaker than me, humans who do not know what I know. I am a god and I'll protect you to the end. Even if fifty bloodthirsty men should stand around us, you will prevail. Rest now. You are about to leave your troubles behind."

She shed sleep on his eyes, then went back to Olympus.

While Odysseus slept, Penelope awoke and, sitting up in bed, started to weep. She prayed to Artemis.

"Artemis, great goddess, daughter of Zeus, fix your arrows in my breast and take away my life, right now. Either that, or may a storm whirl me up and carry me out of here, and throw me down at the mouth of Oceanus, the way stormy winds bore away the daughters of Pandareus, king of Crete. I wish I might pass beneath the hateful earth remembering Odysseus and never have to give pleasure to a baser man. Just tonight I dreamed my husband lay beside me, and I felt glad and I believed it was no dream but that it was really happening."

As she was weeping Odysseus heard her voice. It felt as though she knew him and was standing by him. He gathered up his cloak and the fleeces of his bed, put them on a chair in the hall, and carried the ox hide out to the courtyard. He lifted his hands and prayed to Zeus.

"Father Zeus, if you brought me all this way over land and sea after causing me so much pain, let somebody who's just awakening utter a word of omen, and let there be a sign from you as well."

Zeus heard him and thundered from Olympus, and Odysseus was glad.

Inside the house, the maids were gathering for the morning and laying wood for the fire on the hearth. Telemachus got out of bed and dressed, slinging his sword about his shoulders and binding his sandals on his feet. He took his spear and went into the hall, where he called for Eurycleia. She came immediately.

"Dear nurse," he said, "have you treated the stranger with the appropriate respect? Did you give him a bed and some food? That's typical of the way Mother behaves. She honours the worst kind of stranger, and the better class she sends away."

"Don't blame her, my child," she answered. "He's drunk wine as he wanted and had plenty of food. When he was ready to sleep the maids made up a bed for him in the portico, but he preferred an ox hide and fleeces on the floor. We spread a cloak over him."

Telemachus went out of the palace to the place of assembly to join the other Achaeans.

Eurycleia called out to her maids. "Come now, sweep out the hall, sprinkle the floor with water, then put coverlets on the chairs. Wipe clean the tables and the wine bowls and cups. Some of you go to the spring for water. The suitors will be here soon."

Twenty of the maids went down to the spring while the others worked in the house. The women returned from fetching water, accompanied by Eumaeus. He was driving three boars, which he took out to the courtyard to graze.

"Stranger," he said to Odysseus, "are the suitors still insulting you?"

"Eumaeus, I wish that the gods would take revenge on these men for their wicked acts."

Then they were approached by Melanthius, the goatherd, leading the best goats, followed by two herdsmen. They tied the goats in the courtyard.

"Stranger, are you still here begging for alms?" Melanthius said to Odysseus. "Why don't you go away? I don't think this is likely to end without fisticuffs!"

Odysseus did not reply but just shook his head in silence. A third man came up, Philoetius, leading a heifer and she-goats from the mainland. He tied the animals beneath the portico and went up to Eumaeus.

"Who's the stranger?" he asked. "He looks like a prince – but the gods bring misery on those who wander, even if they are kings."

Philoetius went to Odysseus and extended his right hand.

"Greetings, stranger! May good fortune smile on you, though now you have troubles. Father Zeus brings men into misery. But I swear – when I saw you, my eyes were filled with tears as I thought of Odysseus. He too is probably clothed in rags. I wonder if he's still alive. He put me in charge of his cattle when I was a youth and since then the herd has increased and now strangers eat them whenever they fancy. They do not fear the gods' anger. They want to split between them the possessions of our master who has not been here for years. I would have left long ago, but I still think of that unlucky man, whether perhaps he will come back and drive the suitors out of his house."

"Cowherd, you're no fool, it seems," said Odysseus, "so I will swear you an oath. May Zeus be my witness, Odysseus *will* come home, and you shall see him with your own eyes, killing the suitors who believe they're in charge."

"Stranger, if only Zeus might make this happen!" Philoetius said. "You would find out then how strong my fighting spirit is!"

Eumaeus, too, prayed to the gods that Odysseus might come back.

While they were talking, the suitors, who had assembled in the courtyard, were plotting Telemachus' murder. But a bird flew by them on the left-hand side: an eagle, clutching a dove.

"My friends," said Amphinomus, seeing the omen, "I don't think these plans of ours to kill Telemachus will turn out the way we want. Let's enjoy ourselves at the feast instead!"

The suitors went into the house, put their cloaks on chairs, and fell to killing the sheep and goats, the fat swine and the heifer. They roasted the entrails and mixed wine. Philoetius, the cowherd, gave them bread from a beautiful basket, and Melanthius, the goatherd, poured the wine.

Telemachus seated Odysseus on the stone threshold of the big hall. He set up a shabby stool and a little table and he set out portions of the entrails and poured the wine.

"Sit down here among these lords and drink their wine," he said. "I will ward off any insults. This is not a public house: it is the house of Odysseus!"

Then he spoke loudly to the whole hall.

"As for you suitors, keep your rebukes and your blows to yourself! I don't want any brawling here!"

They bit their lips and marvelled at Telemachus' bold words.

When the flesh of the animals had been roasted and taken from the spits, the portions were divided up. Odysseus was given a serving equal in size to the ones for the suitors, because Telemachus commanded it.

"Hear me, my fellow suitors," said Ctesippus, a wealthy man from a nearby island. "The stranger gets an equal portion, for it is not right to take what is due from Telemachus' guest. But I'll give the stranger a gift too!"

With his strong hand, he hurled the hoof of an ox. Odysseus turned his head sharply and the hoof struck the wall.

"Ctesippus, you missed!" Telemachus said. "That's good, because otherwise I would have stuck my spear right through your middle. Your father would have to host a funeral feast, not a wedding. So let no man – I warn you! – act improperly in my house. But if you want to murder me, that would be better than having to watch constant shameful deeds, strangers being mistreated and men dragging the maids through the hall."

They fell silent, until at last Agelaûs spoke.

"My friends, no man would object to words well spoken. So let's have no more violence towards the stranger, nor to any of the slaves. To Telemachus and his mother I would say just one thing. For as long as everybody hoped that Odysseus would return, no one blamed you for waiting. But Odysseus will not be back, so sit your mother down and tell her that she must choose the best suitor to marry, so that you can enjoy your father's heritage. She should keep another man's house."

"Agelaûs," Telemachus answered, "by Zeus and the sufferings of my father, I am not standing in the way of my mother's marriage. But I don't want to drive her out of the hall against her will. May a god prevent this!"

Suddenly, from nowhere, unquenchable laughter took hold of the suitors. The meat they ate became spattered with blood and their eyes filled with tears and they seemed to be moaning. Theoclymenus the prophet spoke up.

"Ah, you wretches, what horror are you suffering? Your heads are cloaked in night. I hear wailing. You are screaming and these walls are sprinkled with blood. The porch is crowded with ghosts and so is the courtyard – ghosts hurrying down to the House of Hades beneath the darkness. The sun has abandoned the sky and evil shrouds everything."

They laughed merrily.

"This man is mad!" said Eurymachus. "Send him away, since he's convinced that night is here!"

"Eurymachus," said Theoclymenus. "I have eyes, ears, my two feet and a sound mind. I'm going, for I see evil coming your way from which no one will escape."

Theoclymenus left the hall. The suitors started to needle Telemachus.

"Telemachus, no man is more unlucky in his guests than you, with this dirty tramp," said one. And, "He's a burden on the earth. And then this other fellow gets up and prophesizes! You should chuck these strangers

on a ship and send them to Sicily. You might get something for them if you
sold them there."

Telemachus ignored them. In silence, he watched his father, waiting
for the moment when he would lay hands on the suitors.

Penelope had set up a chair opposite the nobles in the main hall and
she heard what each man said. They had made their banquet laughing
freely, a sweet dinner for which they killed many animals. They did not
suspect what banquet awaited them at the hands of Athena and Odysseus!

Book 21

THE CONTEST OF THE BOW

Penelope decided to set up a competition for the suitors, an idea planted in her mind by Athena. She went to the storeroom that held her husband's treasures: bronze, gold and carefully worked iron. Once inside, she located his bow and the quiver full of arrows. This was the bow Odysseus always used when he was in Ithaca.

Penelope took the bow and, weeping as she did so, removed it from its case. Then she went into the main hall. Her maids accompanied her, bearing a chest containing iron axe heads.

"Hear me, you suitors," she cried. "I lay down a challenge: the bow of Odysseus. Whoever strings his bow and shoots an arrow through all twelve axe heads, I will leave with that man, and give up my married home."

Eumaeus and Philoetius wept when they saw their master's bow, but Antinoüs rebuked them.

"Idiots! Why are you crying? Sit down and have something to eat. Or go outside – but leave the bow here. Mind you, I don't think stringing it will be easy."

Secretly, Antinoüs was hoping that he would succeed in stringing the bow himself. In fact, he was the first to taste an arrow from Odysseus' hands.

Telemachus said, "Come on, suitors, give the challenge a go. I will try, too, and prove my right to my father's riches."

Telemachus removed his scarlet cloak and lifted his sword from his shoulders. He dug a trench and lined up the axe heads, tamping the earth down all around them.

Then he attempted to string the bow. Three times it quivered and three times he had to release it. He might have strung it on the fourth attempt, but Odysseus nodded to him to stop.

Telemachus complained. "Maybe I'm just too young. Come now, you who are so much stronger, and begin this contest!"

He leaned the bow against the door and sat down.

"Get up and try, all of you," said Antinoüs. "We'll go from left to right, starting from where the cupbearer pours the wine."

Leiodes stood. He was a soothsayer who hated the foolish behaviour of the other suitors. He took the bow and tried to string it, but without success.

"I can't do it," Leiodes said. "Let somebody else have a go. But I suspect this bow will take many lives."

He placed the bow against the door and sat back down.

"Leiodes," Antinoüs complained, "I don't like this kind of talk! You're saying that this bow is going to rob men of their lives because you can't string it? Your mother bore you too weak to draw a bow. Melanthius, light a fire and bring out a cake of fat so that we can warm the bow and grease it until it's supple."

Melanthius rekindled the fire and brought out a cake of fat. Several of the suitors took it in turns to warm the bow, but they still didn't have the strength to string it.

Meanwhile, Eumaeus and Philoetius and Odysseus went out into the courtyard.

"Philoetius, Eumaeus," said Odysseus. "What kind of men would you be if your master suddenly returned, helped by a god? Would you side with the suitors, or would you help Odysseus?"

"Father Zeus, grant this may happen!" Philoetius answered. "If Odysseus came back, then you would know my full strength!"

Eumaeus said the same.

Then Odysseus announced: "In truth, I'm standing right in front of you!

After great suffering, in the twentieth year, I have returned. If I kill the suitors, I'll give each of you a house near me, and you will be the friends and brothers of Telemachus. Let me show you a sign that proves who I am: the scar I won on Mount Parnassus."

When the men saw the scar, they threw their arms around him and kissed his head and shoulders in welcome. Odysseus kissed their heads and hands in return.

Then he said, "Enough weeping. Somebody may see us. Go inside. The suitors won't allow the bow to be given to me, but as you carry it through the hall, put it in my hands, and instruct the women to bar the doors of the hall. Philoetius, you bar the courtyard gate."

Odysseus entered the house and the two slaves went in as well.

Eurymachus was handling the bow, warming it at the fire, but even so he couldn't string it. Angrily, he groaned, "I'm not that bothered about this marriage anyway. There are plenty of other women. But I regret that we're not measuring up to Odysseus."

Antinoüs replied, "Well, today is the holy feast of Apollo, the archer god. Who would bend a bow on this day? Now sit down! As for the axes, leave them where they are. It's not as if anyone will take them. Come, let's have some wine. In the morning, ask Melanthius to bring the best in his herd so we may lay offerings on the altar of Apollo, the famed archer, and *then* let's try our hands at the bow."

This seemed a good plan. Slaves poured water over their hands and filled their bowls ready for libations, after which they drank to their hearts' content.

Odysseus suddenly spoke up. "I have something to say. To Eurymachus most of all, and to Antinoüs. Give the bow to me so that I may test the strength in my hands, to see if I still have some, as I used to before I became a wanderer."

The suitors became exceedingly angry at his words.

"Ah, wretched stranger, the wine has gone to your head! If you do string the bow, you'll do yourself great harm, for we will send you instantly in a black ship to Echetus, the maimer of men, and you won't escape."

"Antinoüs," Penelope interrupted, "do you think that if the stranger were to string the bow, I would marry him? Certainly not. He doesn't want that, and it wouldn't be seemly."

"Daughter of Icarius, wise Penelope," said Eurymachus, "it's not that we think that this man will take you to his house, but if people hear of this it will damage our reputations. Some common person may say, 'These men cannot string a bow, but a beggar could do it.' This will be a serious stain on us."

"Eurymachus," said Penelope, "is it such a big deal? Give him the bow! If he does string it, I will give him a cloak and tunic and a sharp javelin and a two-edged sword and sandals. And then I'll send him wherever he wants to go."

"Mother," said Telemachus, "no Achaean has more right than I to choose who should be given the bow. None of these men shall thwart my will. So go now to your chamber, Mother, and leave this with me."

Penelope was impressed by his bold words. She went back to her quarters, where she wept for Odysseus until she fell asleep.

Now Eumaeus picked up the bow and all the suitors cried out:

"What are you doing, wretched swineherd? If Apollo is listening, may your own dogs eat you!"

Eumaeus put down the bow, stricken with fear.

"Friend, don't listen to them," Telemachus told Eumaeus. "I wish I were stronger than these suitors. Then I would kick them out for their wicked behaviour."

The suitors laughed merrily, but Eumaeus picked up the bow again and carried it to Odysseus.

Then Eumaeus spoke to Eurycleia in a low voice. "Telemachus asks you to bar the doors of the hall, and if any of the women hear groanings from inside, tell them not to rush in but to remain where they are in silence."

She made no reply but went out and barred the doors of the hall. Philoetius exited the house and barred the gates of the courtyard. He used a ship's cable made of papyrus to fasten them. Then he came back inside.

Odysseus turned the bow around and around, testing it with his hands, fearing that worms might have eaten it.

The suitors glanced at each other and made comments.

"He must be some kind of a connoisseur. Somebody who really knows about bows."

Then, like a singer stretching a new string on a peg of his lyre, who expertly secures the twisted sheep gut, Odysseus strung the bow. He tested the string, and it sang sweetly, like a nightingale. The suitors were horrified. Their faces went pale. Zeus thundered aloud, and Odysseus was glad the great god had given him an omen.

He took up an arrow lying next to him on the table. He laid the arrow on the bridge of the bow, drew back the string and let it fly. He did not miss the holes of the axe heads fixed in the ditch. The arrow went straight through every single one.

"Telemachus," he said, "I think you see that the stranger in your halls does not disgrace you. My strength is still unbroken, whatever the suitors claim. But now it's time for dinner, and a song on my lyre – the long-awaited feast!"

Book 22

SLAUGHTER OF THE SUITORS

Odysseus cast off his rags and sprang over to the threshold with his bow and his quiver.

"Now the contest is won," he said, "let's try another target!"

He aimed an arrow at Antinoüs, raising to his lips a goblet of wine. He was not thinking about death. But Odysseus struck him with the arrow and its tip passed clean through his neck. Antinoüs sank to his side, the cup fell from his hand, and a thick jet of dark red blood gushed out of his nostrils. He thrust the table from him with a kick and spilled the food on the floor.

The suitors broke into uproar. They leapt from their seats and looked along the walls – but there was not a shield or spear anywhere. They railed at Odysseus.

"Stranger, your destruction is guaranteed! Vultures will devour you!"

They thought he had killed Antinoüs by accident, and in their folly did not see their doom approaching.

"You filthy dogs," Odysseus said with an angry glance, "you ravaged my house and assaulted the serving girls and courted my wife. You did not fear the gods or the indignation of men. Now you are ensnared, with no way out."

At his words, fear seized them and each man looked around to see how he might escape.

Eurymachus was the only one to answer. "If you are in fact Odysseus," he replied, "then what you say is right. But Antinoüs was to blame for everything. Antinoüs wanted to kill your son and become king!

"But now Antinoüs is dead, so spare us, and we will repay all that has been drunk and eaten, in bronze and gold."

"Eurymachus," Odysseus answered, "even if you gave me everything you own, I wouldn't refrain from killing you."

Their knees went slack and their courage disappeared.

"Friends," said Eurymachus, "draw your swords, use the tables as shields and let's rush him in a body. Then this fellow will have shot his last arrow."

Eurymachus drew his sword and sprang at Odysseus, but Odysseus let loose an arrow that struck him in the breast. Eurymachus dropped the sword and collapsed over the table, spilling food and wine. He beat the earth with his brow in agony and kicked with his feet, and a dark mist fell over his eyes.

Now Amphinomus rushed at Odysseus. But Telemachus struck him between the shoulders with his spear and drove the weapon through his breast. Amphinomus fell and hit the ground with his forehead. Telemachus jumped back.

"Father, I'll bring you a shield and spears and a helmet," Telemachus said. "As soon as I'm back, I'll arm myself and Eumaeus and Philoetius."

"Run then," Odysseus answered. "Fetch the armour while I still have arrows."

Telemachus rushed to the storeroom and found four shields, eight spears and four helmets with plumes of horsehair. Quickly he carried it all out. He covered his body with the bronze, and Eumaeus and Phloetius put on armour too and took their place at Odysseus' side.

For as long as Odysseus still had arrows, he kept aiming and shooting the suitors, one by one. They fell thick and fast. When the arrows ran out, he took up a shield and placed a helmet on his head. The horsehair plume waved menacingly, a terrible sight. He picked up two stout spears.

Now, set into the wall there was a small postern door raised above ground level, with steps leading up to it. Odysseus could not see it from where he stood.

"My friends," Agelaüs said, "somebody get out through the postern door and raise the alarm with our allies in town."

"I'll go," said Melanthius, the goatherd. "I'll get up to the storehouse and bring you weapons."

Melanthius rushed to the storeroom. He took twelve shields, plenty of spears and many helmets. As fast as he could, he distributed them among the suitors. Odysseus was startled when he saw them donning armour and brandishing spears – suddenly his task seemed even tougher!

"Somebody is working against us," Odysseus said to Telemachus, "I think it's Melanthius."

"Father, it is my fault," Telemachus answered. "I left the storeroom open. Hurry, Eumaeus, and close it."

Melanthius was returning to the storeroom to fetch more armour. This time, Eumaeus spotted him.

"Son of Laertes, Odysseus, there is that bastard going back to the storeroom. Shall I kill him, or bring him to you so that he can pay for his crimes?"

"We'll keep the suitors inside the hall," Odysseus replied. "You grab Melanthius and bind his feet and arms and throw him in the storeroom.

Strap him to a board and hoist him to the roof beams so that he suffers the way he deserves."

Philoetius and Eumaeus went to the storeroom. They lay in wait on either side of the door. When Melanthius came out, the two men jumped him, flinging him to the ground. They bound his feet and hands, then tied his body with a rope and hoisted him to the roof beams.

"Now you can keep watch, here on your soft bed, until dawn arrives," said Eumaeus.

Philoetius and Eumaeus went straight back to Odysseus and his son. The four of them stood on the threshold, breathing fury. But there were many brave men inside the hall.

Athena, disguised as Mentor, came to them.

"Mentor, help us now!" Odysseus pleaded. "Remember, my comrade, how I often helped you!"

Odysseus knew it was Athena, but the suitors shouted out, "Mentor, don't let Odysseus trick you into fighting against us! When we have killed these men, you will be next to die. Then we will take all your possessions, Mentor. We won't allow your sons to live in your halls, nor your daughters, nor your wife!"

"Odysseus," said Mentor, in anger, "where is the courage that you showed against Trojans? How is it, then, that in your own house you weep? No, dear friend, watch what I do, so you may know what kind of man Mentor is when surrounded by the enemy."

So she spoke, but she did not give him the full strength to turn the battle. She flew up to the smoky roof beam in the form of a swallow.

Agelaûs urged on the suitors: "Now even Mentor has deserted him! They are alone by the doors . . . Don't all hurl your spears at once; six of you throw first, aiming for Odysseus. We won't need to worry about the others once he's down."

Agelaûs and six of the suitors hurled their spears, but in vain. One hit the doorpost, another the door. Other spears hit the wall.

"Friends," said Odysseus, "let us throw our spears at the pack!"

They threw their spears with sure aim, each man hitting a suitor, who bit the earth with his teeth. Most of the remaining suitors drew back, but some sprang forwards to pluck the spears from the dead bodies.

They took aim again. One spear hit the doorpost, another the door, another the wall. But Amphimedon hit Telemachus on his wrist, a grazing blow. And Ctesippus grazed Eumaeus' shoulder, but the spear fell to the ground. Once more Odysseus and his company hurled their spears into the throng and again they killed four men. Philoetius hit Ctesippus in the breast.

"Ctesippus, you like to insult people, but where are your big words now? This is your gift, to pay you back for the hoof you gave Odysseus when he was begging in his own house!"

Odysseus wounded another man and so did Telemachus, who thrust his spear into Leiocritus' groin, driving the bronze clean through. Leocritus fell headlong and struck the ground with his forehead.

Then, from up high in the roof, Athena held up her aegis, her shield of victory. The panicked suitors stampeded out of the hall like a herd of cattle attacked by gadfly in spring. And as vultures with their crooked talons and curved beaks come out of the mountains and dart towards the smaller birds that live on the plain, and pounce on them and kill them, and they have no defence or way to escape, Odysseus and his men set on the suitors, killing them left and right, and the floor swam with blood.

Leiodes rushed forwards and clutched Odysseus' knees.

"I beg you, Odysseus," he said, "have pity on me. I have never wronged any of the women! I tried to stop the others whenever they did such things. Is there any gratitude for good behaviour?"

Odysseus replied with an angry glare, "I assume you must have prayed often that I would never return, and that you might marry my wife. So you shall not escape death."

Odysseus seized a sword and struck Leiodes on the neck, and even as the man was speaking his head was mingling with the dust.

Now the singer, Phemius, sought to escape death. He stood holding his lyre near the back door, trying to decide whether to slip out of the hall and sit down by the altar of Zeus in the courtyard, or to rush forwards and clasp Odysseus' knees. He put his lyre down on the ground and rushed forwards and seized Odysseus by the knees.

"I beg you, Odysseus," Phemius said, "to respect me . . . you would be sorry to have killed a singer. The gods have put in my mind all kinds of songs and stories. Telemachus will tell you that I was brought here by force."

"Stay your hand," said Telemachus to his father. "Let Medon go also, a messenger who cared for me when I was a boy."

Medon heard him as he lay huddled beneath a chair. Instantly he rose from his hiding place, took off the ox skin he'd covered himself in, and rushed forwards and clasped Telemachus by the knees.

"My friend," Medon said, "stay your hand and ask your father to stay his. I'm afraid that in his great strength he may harm me with the bronze."

"Take it easy!" Odysseus said. "Telemachus has delivered you. Go and sit down in the court away from the slaughter, you and the singer."

Phemius and Medon went and sat by the altar of Zeus, still anticipating death. Odysseus looked through the hall to see if he had missed anybody, but they were all slaughtered, fallen in the blood and the dust. The suitors lay heaped up like fish drawn from the sea, lying on the curving beach all piled up and longing for the water – but the sun takes away their life.

"Telemachus, call Eurycleia," Odysseus said. "I want to tell her something."

Telemachus rattled the door of the women's quarters and called out.

"Nurse, come out here! Come, my father summons you!"

She opened the doors and came out. She found Odysseus in the middle of the bodies, covered with blood and filth, like a lion who feeds on an ox, his breast and cheeks stained with blood, terrible to see. Eurycleia was ready to raise the cry of celebration, but Odysseus stayed her.

"Be glad in your heart, old woman," said Odysseus, "but hold back for the time being. It is not good to gloat over dead men. The gods have destroyed these suitors for their reckless acts. But come, name for me the women who have betrayed me, and those who are guiltless."

"Certainly, my child," Eurycleia answered. "I will tell you everything. You have fifty women in your house. Of these, twelve have worked against you and your wife Penelope. Now let me go upstairs and tell your wife . . ."

"Don't wake her yet," Odysseus answered, "but bring the shameless women to me."

Eurycleia went to tell the twelve women to come in. Then Odysseus called Telemachus, Philoetius and Eumaeus.

"Carry out the bodies," he said, "and tell the women to clean the chairs and tables with water and sponges. When you've put the house in order, take these twelve women out to the spot in the courtyard between the roundhouse and the wall and cut them down."

The twelve women came in a throng, wailing terribly, shedding tears. First they carried out the dead bodies and set them down beneath the portico. Then they cleaned the chairs and the tables with water and sponges. Telemachus and Eumaeus and Philoetius scraped the floor with hoes and the women carried the scrapings outside. When they had put everything in order inside the hall, Telemachus and the slaves led the women to a narrow place between the roundhouse and the wall of the courtyard from which there was no escape.

Just as when jays or doves fall into a snare in a thicket, trying to reach their nests but finding only a hostile bed, so the women found themselves holding their heads in a row, a noose placed around each woman's neck so that she might die wretchedly.

Then the men led Melanthius out into the courtyard. They cut off his nose and ears and tore out his genitals for the dogs to eat raw, and they cut off his hands and feet. They washed and went back into the house of Odysseus, the work done.

"Bring sulphur, old woman," Odysseus said to Eurycleia, "so we can cleanse the pollution. And bring me fire so I can purge the hall. Then tell Penelope to come here and order the women in the house to come too."

"Yes, my child," said Eurycleia, "but let me bring you a cloak and a tunic so that you do not stand here wrapped in rags."

"First of all make a fire for me in the hall," Odysseus answered.

Eurycleia obeyed, and she brought fire and sulphur, which Odysseus used to fumigate the hall. Eurycleia went back to tell the women to come in. They entered with torches and thronged around Odysseus, embracing him, and kissing his head and shoulders and hands. He felt like crying because he was so overjoyed to see them.

Book 23

REUNION AT LAST

The old nurse hurried to the upper chamber to give Penelope the news that her husband had at last come home. She shuffled so fast her elderly legs trembled as she stood by the lady's bed.

"Wake up, dear child!" Eurycleia said. "Wake up and see what you have awaited so long! Odysseus is here! He's killed the suitors!"

"Dear nurse," Penelope said, "the gods are driving you mad. Making up this wild story, rousing me from a deep sleep! If any of the other women told me this, I would have sent her packing with a punishment. But I forgive you because of your old age."

"I am not joking, dear child!" Eurycleia replied. "Odysseus is here. He is the stranger the suitors would not respect!"

Penelope jumped out of bed and threw her arms around Eurycleia, letting tears flood out.

"Dear nurse," Penelope said, "Has he really come home as you say, and killed the suitors – even though he was all alone and they were in a huge gang?"

"I didn't see it happen," Eurycleia said. "I heard the groaning of the men being killed. All the women sat terrified in the inner part of the house until Telemachus called me. Then I discovered Odysseus standing in the middle of the dead bodies all piled high. The sight would have warmed your heart. Now the bodies have been gathered up and he has sent me to call you. So come with me! The two of you can enjoy a wonderful reunion. You've suffered so much, but your long-held wish has been granted."

"Dear nurse," she said, "you know how welcome the sight of him would be. But it's the gods who have killed the suitors, angry at their insolence. Odysseus is still lost, somewhere far off."

"My child," Eurycleia replied, "Your heart is stubborn. I'll give you proof. The scar that Odysseus received from a boar – I saw it when I washed his feet. I wanted to tell you, but he covered my mouth with his hand. So come with me, and if you find I have deceived you, then kill me, in as cruel a way as you wish."

"Dear nurse," Penelope answered, "it is hard to understand the will of the gods. Let us go so that I can see the dead suitors, and the man who killed them."

Penelope went down from the upper chamber, wondering whether she should stand aloof and question her husband, or whether she should go to him and clasp him and kiss his head and hands.

When she entered the hall she sat down opposite Odysseus. She remained silent for a long time.

"My hard-hearted mother!" Telemachus said. "Why do you hold yourself aloof? You see your husband come home, and yet remain silent. Your heart is made of stone!"

"My child, my heart is lost in wonder," she answered. "I can barely speak or look him in the eye. But if he really is Odysseus, we will know one another. We have secret signs, unknown to others."

Odysseus smiled. "Telemachus, let your mother test me and she will see more clearly. Right now I'm filthy and wearing shabby clothes, so she cannot tell who I am.

"But we need to think about the situation we're in. When a man kills someone, he's sent into exile by the dead man's relatives. We have killed many men, and the noblest Ithacans at that. We have to make a plan."

"You take care of this, dear father," Telemachus answered. "They say that you are the smartest man alive. We'll follow and obey you."

"This is what we should do," Odysseus answered. "Everybody take a bath. Put on clean tunics – tell the handmaids to choose fine clothes. Instruct the musicians to play music for a dance. That way, neighbours who hear the noise will believe that a wedding feast is taking place and the rumour of the killing of the suitors will not spread. Meanwhile we can retreat to the farm, where we can devise whatever plans Zeus makes possible."

They did as he said. Odysseus went into the bathing room and Eurynomê bathed him. She anointed him with oil, dressed him in a tunic and threw a cloak about his shoulders. Athena shed beauty over his head, and she made his locks flow in curls like a hyacinth's. The goddess bestowed grace on Odysseus the way a skilled craftsman, tutored by Hephaestus and Athena, overlays silver with gold.

He came out of the bath like a god and sat down again on the chair opposite his wife.

"Incredible lady! No other woman would stay distant from a husband who after huge suffering had come, in the twentieth year, to his home."

"It is you who are incredible," Penelope replied, "But I'm not as astonished by you now as I was before. You look as you did when you departed from Ithaca on your ship. Come, Eurycleia, bring our bed from the bridal chamber, the one he made with his own hands. Bring it out for him to lie on."

"Woman," Odysseus said, in sudden anger, "who has messed with the bed I built? No mortal could pry it from its place! There was an olive tree growing in the court, vigorous, and sturdy as a pillar. I built my chamber around this tree and trimmed the trunk and fashioned it into the bedpost. I sanded the timbers, then decorated it with gold and silver and ivory. Woman, is my bedstead still in its place, or has some man cut the trunk of the olive tree?"

Penelope's knees went weak, and her heart melted as she recognized the sign. She burst into sobs and ran towards Odysseus and threw her arms about his neck and kissed his face.

"Odysseus, don't be angry," she said. "I was afraid that some man or god would come in your likeness and trick me. But you know about our bed, which no other man has ever seen. You have convinced me."

A desire to weep rose up in him. He held her in his arms, his beloved wife. As the sight of land is welcome to men whose ship has been wrecked by wind and waves – the few men who have made their escape by swimming, bodies crusted with brine, and gladly set foot on land – so Penelope was welcome to her husband, as she gazed on him and could not loosen her arms from his neck.

"My wife, our troubles aren't over yet," Odysseus said. "There is still work ahead. The spirit of Teiresias told me so when I went to the House of Hades. But come, let us go to bed, my wife, so that we may take our joy."

"Your bed is ready whenever you wish," Penelope said. "But tell me of the trouble to come. It's better that I know."

"I will tell you everything. Teiresias told me to travel around carrying an oar on my shoulder until I came to men who know nothing of the sea, who eat food unmixed with salt and know nothing of ships. He told me that when a wayfarer asks why I have a winnowing fan on my shoulder, then I should fix my oar in the earth, make offerings to Poseidon – a ram, a bull, a boar – then go back home and sacrifice animals to the gods.

He said that death will come to me away from the sea, when sleek old age overcomes me and my people are prosperous."

"Well, if the gods are going to bring you a happy old age, there is hope!" Penelope replied.

So they spoke to one another, and Eurycleia and Eurynomê prepared the bed, then Eurynomê led them to the bridal chamber. They gave in to joy in the ancient ritual.

When the two had had their fill of love-making, they took delight in speaking to each other. Penelope told Odysseus how she had endured the suitors. He recounted all the woes he had inflicted on other men, and all that he'd suffered, too. Then Athena brought on Dawn, and Odysseus rose from the bed.

"Wife, we've both endured many troubles," he said to Penelope, "but now you must look after the riches inside the house. I need to go to the farm to see my father. Be careful. Now that the sun is up, reports will leak that we have killed the suitors. So go to your chamber and sit there. Do not look out or ask questions of anybody."

Odysseus put on his armour, and Telemachus and Philoetius and Eumaeus did too. They went out of the house. Odysseus led the way. By now light had come over the earth, but Athena hid them in night and led them from the city.

Book 24

PEACE RESTORED

Hermes summoned the ghosts of the suitors from the house. They followed him, gibbering the way bats gibber in the recess of a cave. Hermes led them down dark paths, past the streams of Oceanus and the White Rocks and the Gates of the Sun and the Land of Dreams. They reached the Meadow of Asphodel where ghosts dwell.

Here they found the ghosts of Achilles and Patroclus. Approaching them was the ghost of Agamemnon, surrounded by the souls of all those who died with him.

Achilles addressed him. "Agamemnon, we thought you were favoured above all others by Zeus. How much better it would have been if you had died on the plain at Troy. The Achaeans would have built you a tomb, and you would have been bathed in glory. Instead, you met a piteous death."

"You lucky, Achilles, to have died at Troy," Agamemnon said. "We battled long and hard and carried your body to the ships and placed you on a bier and cleaned your flesh with warm water and ointment. And your mother Thetis came out of the sea with the nymphs when she heard what had happened, and a great cry arose over the deep.

"Then the daughters of the Old Man of the Sea clothed you with immortal clothing, and the Muses sang a song. For seventeen days, night and day, we cried for you, and on the eighteenth we gave you to the fire. We killed fat sheep and cattle, and you were burned in the clothing with an abundance of unguents and honey. When you were burned we gathered your white bones and put them in a golden jar that Thetis gave us, with unmixed wine and oils, and we mingled your bones with those of dear departed Patroclus. We built a tomb on the headland of the Hellespont that could be seen from far distant.

"Your mother asked the gods for beautiful prizes, which she displayed in the middle of the competition ground. You've attended many such games following the death of a king when the young men compete to win rewards, but if you'd seen these prizes you would have been amazed – they were extraordinary.

"As for me, I met a bitter doom at the hands of my cousin Aegisthus and his lover, my wife Clytemnestra!"

Hermes came to them leading the ghosts of the suitors. Agamemnon recognized Amphimedon, who had entertained him at his home in Ithaca.

"Amphimedon, what has happened?" Agamemnon asked. "You've come beneath the earth, you and Ithaca's other nobles. Did Poseidon destroy you on board ship? Or did the enemy harm? Tell me – I'm a friend of your house!"

"Great Agamemnon," said the ghost of Amphimedon, "we were courting the wife of Odysseus and she neither refused us nor accepted. Then some god brought Odysseus home. He met Telemachus, returning from Pylos. Together they planned our death. He came in disguise and asked his wife to set up a challenge, to string Odysseus' bow and fire an arrow through the holes in twelve axe heads. But none of us could string the bow. When Odysseus got hold of it, he strung it with ease before shooting an arrow through the axe heads.

"Then he stood on the threshold and let all the arrows fly, and the men fell thick and fast. Some god was obviously on his side.

"So we all died, Agamemnon, and our bodies lie uncared for because our friends know nothing of what has happened."

So spoke the ghost of Amphinomus.

"Oh fortunate Odysseus, truly excellent was the wife he won!" said the ghost of Agamemnon. "Clever, clever, clever Penelope, daughter of Icarius! She kept the image of Odysseus, her husband, faithfully in mind! Not like the daughter of Tyndareus, Clytemnestra, my wife, who plotted her husband's murder in a conspiracy with Aegisthus."

So the ghosts spoke as they stood in the House of Hades beneath the dark earth.

Odysseus and his men arrived at the well-ordered farm of Laertes. There was a house there, and outbuildings where his slaves ate and slept. Inside the house was an old Sicilian woman who took care of Laertes. The slaves were sitting out front, on benches.

"Go ahead into the house," Odysseus said. "I want to see my father and find out whether he recognizes me."

Odysseus went to the rich vineyard. He discovered his father, alone, digging around a plant. He wore a dirty patched tunic and shin guards of ox hide to protect against scratches. On his hands he wore gloves, and his head was covered by a goatskin cap. When Odysseus saw him so worn with old age, and ruined by grief, he stood quietly beneath a tall pear tree and wept.

Then he went up to his father.

"Old man, I think you know how to tend a garden. I don't see any plant that lacks care, not a fig tree or vine, no, nor a single olive in the field. Let me tell you something else too, though, but don't be offended . . . you, in contrast, don't receive such care! You suffer a bitter old age and wear tattered clothes. You don't appear to be a slave; in fact you have the air of a king!

"Whose orchard do you tend? And is this Ithaca? In my native land I once hosted a man who said he came from Ithaca. He told me his father was Laertes. Well, I took him into the house and entertained him and gave him riches from my store: seven bars of gold and a mixing bowl of silver, and twelve cloaks and many blankets and as many tunics, and fine women of his choice, also, skilled at weaving."

"Stranger," Laertes answered, "you have come to the country that you asked about, but it is now ruled over by arrogant and brutal men. And you gave those gifts in vain. If you had found that man still alive, he would have sent you on your way with hospitality and entertainment.

"But come, how many years is it since you entertained this unfortunate guest, my son? The fish have devoured him now, or he has become prey for beasts and birds along the shoreline.

"Tell me . . . who are you? And where do you come from? Where's your city and who are your parents? Where's your ship that brought you here?"

"I will tell you everything," Odysseus answered. "I come from Alybas, 'Wanderer Town', where I live in a famous house. I'm the son of Apheidas, 'Unsparing', and my name is Eperitus, 'Watcher'. A god drove me here against my will. My ship lies over there, away from the city. As for Odysseus, it's been five years since he left. He had birds of good omen when he set out and he was in good spirits and we looked forward to meeting again and exchanging gifts."

A black cloud of grief came over Laertes. With both his hands he scooped up the dust and poured it over his head, groaning. Odysseus' heart was broken as he looked at his father. He sprang towards him and wrapped him in his arms and kissed him.

"I am that man, father," Odysseus said. "I have come back to my native land. Stop your grief. I've killed the suitors and taken revenge for their outrage."

"If you are really Odysseus, my son, then show me some sign."

"This scar, look," Odysseus answered, "given to me by a boar on Parnassus. And I will tell you about the trees that you gave me when I followed you through the garden as a child. We passed through these very ones, and you named them and told me about them: you gave me thirteen pear trees and ten apple trees and forty fig trees and rows of vines, around fifty."

His father felt faint as he recognized the tokens, and he threw his arms around his son.

"Father Zeus, you gods do indeed hold sway on Olympus," Laertes said, "if the suitors have paid for their crimes. But I'm afraid that now their relatives will rally against us for revenge."

"Don't worry father," Odysseus answered. "We'll take care of it. Let's go into the house. I sent Telemachus there with the goatherd and swineherd to prepare a meal."

They went into the house and found Telemachus, Philoetius and Eumaeus carving meat and mixing the wine.

The Sicilian handmaid bathed Laertes and anointed him and cast a cloak around his shoulders. Athena came and made Laertes' limbs taller and stronger so that when he came out of the bath Odysseus was amazed to see him.

"Father, I think that a god has made you more excellent to behold," Odysseus said.

"I only wish I had the strength I had as a young man and had stood by your side when you killed the suitors."

They sat down for the meal. Just then an old slave named Dolius from Penelope's household came into the house with his sons. The Sicilian woman had called them in. Dolius was astounded to see Odysseus and ran towards him with outstretched arms. He clasped Odysseus' hands and kissed them.

"Odysseus, my master, you have come back to us – hail and welcome! May the gods grant you happiness! And tell me, does Penelope know you are here?"

"Old man, she knows!"

The sons of Dolius gathered around Odysseus and greeted him in the same way.

In the meantime, Rumour, the messenger, travelled swiftly through the city telling of the suitors' terrible deaths. At once the people congregated, moaning and wailing, in front of Odysseus' house. They carried the dead out. Then, very mournful, they gathered in the place of assembly. Eupeithes stood up, for he grieved the loss of his son Antinoüs.

"My friends, truly a monstrous deed has been done," Eupeithes said. "Odysseus took our men off in his ships and he lost them all, and now he's killed others. It would be a disgrace not to avenge the deaths of our sons and brothers!"

Then Medon, whom Odysseus had spared, addressed them.

"Hear me, men of Ithaca! Odysseus has done this through the will of the gods. I myself saw a god appear in front of Odysseus and give him strength as he raged through the halls."

Fear seized them. Then Halitherses spoke, a friend to Odysseus and a prophet.

"Listen to me now! You would not obey me, nor Mentor, and make your sons stop this insanity. They committed a monstrous deed by frittering away Odysseus' wealth and dishonouring his wife. So let it be. Let us not go after him, or we will bring more disasters upon ourselves."

Half of them sprang up crying out loud. They did not like his speech. The other half stayed in their seats. The first half rushed to arm themselves.

They congregated outside the city, led by Eupeithes, who hoped to avenge the killing of his son Antinoüs.

Athena spoke to Zeus.

"Father of all, son of Cronus, what are you planning now? Are you going to bring about more war and slaughter?"

"My child, why do you ask me?" Zeus said. "Weren't you the one who concocted this plan? Now that Odysseus has had his revenge on the suitors, let them swear that he will be king for all his days, and we shall prompt them to love one another. Let wealth and peace be theirs!"

Athena darted down from Olympus.

The men in the hut finished eating.

"Somebody go outside and see whether the suitors' relatives are coming," Odysseus said.

One of Dolius' sons went to look and saw the men were close at hand.

"They're near!" he said. "We must prepare!"

They donned their armour. Odysseus had four men, the sons of Dolius were six, and Laertes and Dolius made up twelve, although they were grey-haired. Athena appeared in the guise of Mentor, and Odysseus was happy to see her.

"Telemachus," Odysseus said, "now you can learn how to fight in an important battle. Don't bring disgrace on your father's house. Be great in strength!"

"You will see me doing the right thing, dear father! There will be no disgrace on your house!"

Laertes was delighted. "I rejoice that my son and my son's son quarrel over which of them is bravest."

Athena breathed strength into Laertes. He prayed to Athena, raised his spear, hurled it and struck Eupeithes, in spite of his helmet with its cheek-pieces of bronze. The spear passed through it, and Eupeithes collapsed with a thud, his armour clanging around him.

Then Odysseus and his son fell on the front line of fighters with swords and spear. They would have killed them all had not Athena shouted aloud, "Stop! Be parted without bloodshed!"

Pale fear seized the Achaeans, and they dropped their weapons and turned towards the city, desperate to save their lives. Odysseus gave a terrible cry and gathered himself together and swooped on them like an eagle. But Zeus at that very moment released a flaming thunderbolt that fell directly in front of Athena.

"Son of Laertes, sprung from Zeus, artful Odysseus," Athena said, "see the sign my father sends you. Stop this battle now so that Zeus will not become angry with you."

Odysseus was glad to obey. And so Athena brought peace to the island of Ithaca, where Odysseus returned as King.

First published in 2026
by Riverside Press, an imprint of

UniPress Books Ltd
World's End Studios
London SW10 0RJ
United Kingdom

ISBN: 978-1-917226-39-4
ISBN e-book: 978-1-917226-40-0

This book is distributed throughout the UK and Europe
by Abrams & Chronicle Books, 1 West Smithfield, London,
EC1A 9JU and 57 rue Gaston Tessier, 75166 Paris, France.

www.abramsandchronicle.co.uk
info@abramsandchronicle.co.uk

Commissioning Editor: Claire Collins
Associate Publisher: Daniel Mills
Art direction and cover design: Alexandre Coco
Designer: Luke Herriott
Front cover image: Joanna Lisowiec
With thanks to Kathleen Steeden

Printed in China
riversidepress.co.uk

1 2 3 4 5 6 7 8 9 10